GETTING INTO COLLEGE

Pat Ordovensky
Education Writer
USA TODAY

 Peterson's
Princeton, New Jersey

Library of Congress Cataloging-in-Publication Data

Ordovensky, Pat.
    Getting into college / Pat Ordovensky.
      p.   cm.
    At head of title: USA today.
    Includes index.
    ISBN 1-56079-463-1
    1. Universities and colleges—United States—Admission. 2. Universities and Colleges—United States—Entrance requirements. I. USA today (Arlington, Va.) II. Title.
LB2351.2.072 1995
378.1'056'0973—dc20   95-12443
                                           CIP

Interior design by CDS Design
Cover illustration by Patrick Merrell

Printed in the United States of America

10 9 8 7 6 5 4 3 2 1

Visit Peterson's Education Center on the Internet (World Wide Web) at http://www.petersons.com

TABLE OF CONTENTS

Acknowledgments

Every writer who has accepted money for putting words on paper hopes that some day a task will come that is more fun than work. For me, this book is it. In the 15 years that I have been dealing with college officials as an education writer for Gannett News Service and *USA TODAY*, I have collected thousands of bits of information in my head and elsewhere about the college admission process. When *USA TODAY* and Peterson's asked me to write this book, it was a chance to pull all those facts from their hiding places and present them in a coherent manner.

I welcomed the opportunity to write this book because those assembled facts form a picture every student should see. They show that getting into college is not a mystery-shrouded event. It's simply a matter of two entities, a student and a college, deciding if they like each other well enough to spend some time together.

My thanks go to hundreds of college officials, high school counselors, students, and parents who, over the years, have contributed to my education. Their names are too numerous, and some too forgotten, to mention. But I must specifically thank William Conley, Dean of Undergraduate Admissions at Case Western Reserve and Frank Burtnett, Executive Director of *Education Now* who read this manuscript to check its accuracy. Both gentlemen reminded me of a fact or two I had forgotten.

Deans of Admission Lee Stetson at the University of Pennsylvania, Ted O'Neill at the University of Chicago, Bruce Poch at Pomona College, Cliff Sjogran then at the University of Michigan, and others who have allowed me to enter their lairs, talk to their staffs, and listen to their deliberations deserve a special mention. They permitted me to watch as students' essays were criticized, high schools compared, and letters of recommendation read between the lines.

Since 1988, invaluable information has come from the hundreds of officials who volunteer to answer phones each year on *USA TODAY*'s College Admission/Financial Aid Hotline. For three days every October they share their expertise with thousands of students and parents and, in the process, with this reporter. After the 1994 hotline, Gary Ripple of Lafayette College and Jim Walters of the University of North Carolina–Chapel Hill graciously brought me up to date on some current aspects of the admission process.

At CASE (Council for Advancement and Support of Education), which cosponsors the hotline, Brett Chambers, Kim Hughes, and Lisa Hatem have met the annual challenge of recruiting and scheduling experts. Without them there would be neither hotline nor book.

The guiding spirit pushing this book to reality, as he is with so many *USA TODAY* projects, was Bob Dubill, the newspaper's executive editor who also served as No. 1 consultant on the parent's perspective. Bob and son Andrew probably hold the world record for campuses visited (25) in the college-selection process. (Andrew went to Princeton.)

Also contributing at *USA TODAY* were Lynn Perri and her corps of graphic artists and Carol Skalski who can turn chaos into order by waving her hand.

At Peterson's, editor Carol Hupping uncannily thinks of facts I have forgotten and reminds me to remember them.

If the words in this book make sense to you, we both must thank the late George Starr Lasher, an Ohio University professor who taught me more than anyone else about the discipline required to communicate in written English. It is to my alma mater's everlasting shame that it dropped his tough courses when he retired.

And of course I must thank my wife, Mary Ann, who tolerates my strange habit of spending the beautiful days of Sarasota, Florida in front of a computer punching keys. May she never cease complaining that I learned all this good stuff about colleges too late to help our kids.

Pat Ordovensky

CHAPTER ONE

SO YOU'RE GOING TO COLLEGE

. . . getting there doesn't have to be a pain

It's like death and taxes. You know it's coming, but when it arrives you're not ready.

You've known for a long time that someday you, or your kids, will be going to college. Now someday is almost here. It's time to look for a college and find the money to pay for it.

You're suddenly confused. Questions swarm through your head and you're not sure where to go for answers.

How do you find a college? How do you know it's the right one? How do you know that when you pick a college it will want you as a student? Why are colleges sending you stuff you didn't ask for? If you find the right college, how will you afford it?

As you start asking the questions, the confusion increases. Your school counseling center has large directories with hundreds of pages of small print telling you more than you want to know about every college that ever awarded a degree. What does it all mean?

Your library has a computer program that tells you which colleges offer certain majors, which are in large cities and small towns, which have more women than men, which are big on fraternities and sororities, and dozens of other facts that probably are important. But where do you start?

If you're a good student, fancy brochures with photos of smiling teenagers on pastoral campuses are showing up in your mailbox from colleges you've never heard of. Why are they telling you about their schools when they don't even know you? A company offers video clips depicting life on certain campuses. Is it worth the money?

Your friends and their parents who have just gone through the finding-a-college experience are relating horror stories about the trauma involved, the reams of forms to be filled out, the essays to be written, the miles traveled visiting campuses, the pain of baring your soul on a financial aid application.

You've even heard about parents and kids in shouting matches over choosing a college. Do you need all this?

This book is written as pain relief. It's the aspirin, if you will, for the getting-into-college headache. It will take you on a step-by-step stroll through the process and show that, taking it one step at a time, there need not be any pain. Hey, it might even be fun.

MAYBE YOU'RE NOT A KID

Maybe you're an older, mature adult. Maybe you're what the educators call a nontraditional student, which is their jargon for anyone over 24.

Maybe you just lost your job, are having trouble finding another, and think it's time to go to college to acquire new skills. Maybe the kids just left the nest and you're ready to return to that long-ago-interrupted pursuit of a degree. Maybe you're just seeking a new challenge.

If that's you, you're hardly alone. Thousands of adults enroll in colleges, either for the first time or as returnees, every year. For them, the process can be more bewildering and painful than for younger students. They're often intimidated by their age and then surprised to find colleges eagerly welcoming them.

This book offers adult aspirin, too. At the end of many chapters, including this one, it will retrace the step-by-step stroll for students who aren't kids. If there is no special section for adult students, the entire chapter applies to students of all ages.

WHAT YOU NEED TO KNOW

Let's start with some facts. There are more than 3,200 colleges in the United States. Of them, a bit more than half offer four-year bachelor's degrees. About 500 are public four-year colleges, subsidized by the states in which they're located. Almost all the rest are private institutions that rely chiefly on their endowments, tuition, and fund-raising appeals for money. Five are run by the federal government to train military officers, and their students are paid stipends to attend. Most of the large research universities are public. Most of the small liberal arts colleges are private.

There are more than 3,200 colleges in the United States; a bit more than half offer four-year bachelor's degrees.

A large group of private colleges are sponsored, and in some cases partially supported, by religious denominations. Notre Dame (Catholic), Brigham Young (Mormon), and Baylor (Baptist) are among the better-known colleges with religious ties.

Public colleges are much less expensive than private colleges because their state subsidies keep their tuition down. But the best rates are available only to residents of their states. All state colleges assess a surcharge to out-of-staters that pushes their costs to private-school levels.

Private colleges, as a rule, have much more money to give away in financial aid than state-supported schools. Some budget up to 30 percent of their income to help students pay their bills.

When it comes to accepting students, colleges fall into three distinct categories:

- Open admission: They'll accept anyone with a high school diploma or its equivalent until they're full. Some state colleges and most two-year colleges are required by law to take any graduate of a high school in their state.
- Rolling admission: They consider applications, and accept or reject them, as they arrive. Early applicants who meet these schools' academic criteria have a better chance than those who apply late.
- The Ivy League model (also called May 1 schools): They accept their entire freshman class at the same time, usually in late March or early April, and give students until May 1 to decide if they'll enroll.

A final fact, for now: At this moment, you are one of 2.5 million people looking for a college. Among them are 20,664 high school seniors who will become their class valedictorians.

That's a number to ponder. There are enough valedictorians each year to fill the freshman classes at the eight Ivy League colleges, Duke, Stanford, and the University of Chicago and have about 3,500 left over.

You're probably not a valedictorian. But if you're looking for a college, you're in good company. Good luck.

WHERE TO START

A colossal mass of information—books, directories, software programs—exists to help college-bound students make wise decisions. No one can possibly digest all of it. But much of it can be useful in identifying the colleges that might be right for you. The trick is to know the difference between the information you need and don't need.

The best way to start is by making a list. Write down variables that go into selecting a college; then decide how important each is to you. Let's begin with the most obvious:

Distance

Do you want to leave home? Do you look forward to college as an opportunity to flee the nest and live independently? Or would you be more comfortable staying home while you cope with the challenge of handling college work?

If you're ready to leave, how far would you like to go? Is it essential to come home on weekends or once a month? Do you want to get out of your hometown but stay close enough to keep in touch with family and friends? Can you survive seeing your family only at Thanksgiving, Christmas, and Spring Break?

Can you handle a climate change? If you live in the South and go to college in the North, can you cope with cold temperatures and snow?

Think about each question. Then think how strongly you feel about each an-

> **Do you look forward to college as an opportunity to flee the nest or would you be more comfortable staying home?**

FACTORS IN THE FIRST CUT

Here's the list of items to consider in making your first list of colleges that might fit you. Rank them in their order of importance to YOU.

Distance. How far from home do you want to be?

Size. Are you more comfortable at a large, small, or medium-sized campus?

Location. Do you prefer a big city, the suburbs, or a rural environment?

Majors. Do you know what your major will be?

Housing. Do you care if most students live on campus?

Students. Single sex or coed? A campus where one race or religious denomination is dominant?

Academic Rigor. Do you want to be the smartest student on campus? Or among the average?

Cost. It's not an important factor until you learn how much financial aid you will get.

swer. If your feelings are strong, one way or the other, write "distance" on your list as a variable to be considered. If you don't really care how far you go, it's not a factor.

Size

Ohio State has 33,000 undergraduates. Ohio Dominican has 900. They have two things in common: they offer an excellent education and are in Columbus, Ohio. Each is the right choice for some students but neither is right for all students.

Ohio State and Ohio Dominican are on opposite ends of the size spectrum. Colleges, public and private, can be found in all sizes. Is size important to you? Think about it.

Would you feel more comfortable swimming in a small pond or

> **Would you feel more comfortable swimming in a small pond or mingling with the masses in the ocean?**

mingling with the masses in the ocean? Are small classes with more individual instruction, usually prevalent on smaller campuses, a desirable feature? Could you accept huge classes, where you're likely to be just a number, for the wide variety of activities, culture, and social life that a major university offers? Or do you lean toward a medium-sized campus of 5,000 to 10,000 students where you get some of each world? If your feelings are strong, write "size" on your list.

Majors

If you know what you want to study, this is important. If you plan to major in chemistry, you want a college that offers a chemistry major. If you're undecided but leaning toward certain fields, put them on your list. You can decide later, as you gather information, how heavily to weigh a college's academic offerings in making your decision.

If you are totally at sea over the choice of a major, leave it off your list and don't worry about it. You'll have plenty of company among your classmates wherever you go. Many colleges, recognizing this widespread indecision, don't require students to select a major until their second or third year.

Housing

Do you want to live on campus? Are you fussy about a single-sex or coed dorm? Would you like a school where a large majority of students live in dorms? Or do you mind if most of them commute from home each day?

Most colleges can be classified either as residential or commuter, with at least two thirds of their students in one of the two categories. But some strike an even balance between on-campus and live-at-home students. Is it important?

Students

Do you feel strongly about the type of students who'll be your classmates? Would you like to be on a campus where your sex dominates? Or where you're outnumbered by the opposite sex? Or would you like an even balance?

Are you interested in being challenged, or would you be more comfortable where the SAT/ACT average is the same as yours?

Is racial and ethnic diversity important? If you're African American, would you prefer a predominantly black campus? How about geographic diversity? Some colleges get more than 90 percent of their students from their own states.

Academic Rigor

This one's difficult to measure because the only yardstick doesn't work well. The widely accepted, if not totally valid, gauge of a school's academic toughness is its students' average scores on the SAT or ACT college admission tests.

Do you feel strongly about the test scores of your classmates? Are you interested in being challenged by students who score higher than you? Would you be more comfortable on a campus where the SAT/

THE TOUGHEST TICKETS

A college's low acceptance rate, which means many students are applying for few spots, can be produced by many things, The nation's two lowest—Missouri's College of the Ozarks and New York's Cooper Union—are popular because they charge no tuition. Others get many applications because of their prestige among high school students. These 24 colleges accepted fewer than 35 percent of their applicants for 1994–95.

College	Percent Accepted
College of the Ozarks, Point Lookout, MO (no tuition)	7%
Cooper Union, New York, NY (no tuition)	13%
Harvard University, Cambridge, MA	14%
Princeton University, Princeton, NJ	14%
Yale University, New Haven, CT	19%
Amherst College, Amherst, MA	20%
Stanford University, Stanford, CA	20%
Brown University, Providence, RI	22%
Rice University, Houston, TX	22%
Dartmouth College, Hanover, NH	23%
Georgetown University, Washington, DC	24%
California Institute of Technology, Pasadena, CA	25%
Columbia College, New York, NY	25%
Williams College, Williamstown, MA	27%
Washington and Lee University, Lexington, VA	29%
Bowdoin College, Brunswick, ME	30%
Duke University, Durham, NC	30%
Massachusetts Institute of Technology, Cambridge, MA	30%
Swarthmore College, Swarthmore, PA	30%
Berea College, Berea, KY	30%
Middlebury College, Middlebury, VT	32%
Pomona College, Claremont, CA	32%
Cornell University, Ithaca, NY	33%
Bates College, Lewiston, ME	34%

Source: Peterson's Guides, Inc.

ACT average is the same as your score? Or would you like the big fish role at a campus where most students didn't do as well as you?

If any of these options evoke a strong response, write "SAT/ACT" or "test score" or "rigor" on your list.

Cost

It should go on your list of items to consider but at the bottom. How much you pay certainly will be a factor in your decision but should not, at this early stage, be an overriding concern.

The sticker shock will be real when you see some colleges' published tuition. Shake it off and get on with more important thoughts. The reality of today's market is that most students don't pay the sticker price. Financial aid from governments, private sources, and colleges themselves is available to reduce the blow.

Find the colleges that fit you best, regardless of cost, and compare aid offers later.

When the time comes to apply to the colleges you've selected, you also will submit an application for financial aid. Each college that accepts you will tell you how much aid you'll get if you enroll.

Many schools, usually higher-priced private colleges, offer sizable tuition discounts to lure students they really want. It's a buyer's market, because the pool of high school graduates is smaller than the number of spots in college freshman classes, and it will remain so for the next few years.

You are the buyer and if a college wants you, it will tell you so with money. I'll talk about getting the discounts and other financial aid in Chapter Eight.

For now, money is not a major concern because you're not sure how much you'll have to pay. Find the colleges that fit you best, regardless of cost. Later, when you have been accepted by your top choices, you can weigh their financial aid offers in deciding where you'll go. That's when cost becomes a factor.

THE TOP TEST SCORES

Most colleges now report SAT scores in ranges, usually the middle 50 percent of entering freshmen. These schools' freshmen had the highest SAT ranges in 1994–95. It means 25 percent of the students scored higher than the higher number, 25 percent scored lower than the lower number.

College	25 Percent Score Higher	25 Percent Score Lower
Harvard & Radcliffe Colleges	1490	1310
California Institute of Technology	1490	1320
Massachusetts Institute of Technology	1470	1290
Yale University	1460	1250
Princeton University	1460	1280
Harvey Mudd College	1460	1290
Columbia College	1450	1250
Williams College	1450	1250
Duke University	1440	1250
Rice University	1440	1210
Stanford University	1440	1190
Amherst College	1430	1240
Cooper Union	1420	1230
Dartmouth College	1420	1240
Pomona College	1420	1240
Wesleyan University	1410	1210
Brown University	1410	1190
Swarthmore College	1410	1210
Johns Hopkins University	1400	1200
Northwestern University	1400	1200
University of Chicago	1400	1200
University of Pennsylvania	1390	1200
Cornell University	1380	1180
Haverford College	1380	1200
Carleton College	1380	1170
Case Western Reserve University	1370	1120
University of California-Berkeley	1370	1090
Reed College	1360	1120
Carnegie Mellon University	1360	1130
Grinnell College	1360	1150
Bard College	1360	1100
University of Notre Dame	1360	1160

Source: USA TODAY research, The College Board

Important Facts: Once again for emphasis I am repeating two sentences written above. They will be repeated throughout these pages because they're important facts to remember:

- Most students don't pay the published sticker price.
- Many colleges offer sizable tuition discounts to lure students they really want.

The No. 1 factor in making you an attractive student is an excellent academic record. So your high school report card can have as much influence on your tuition as it does on being accepted by a college.

EASY, WASN'T IT?

You have just taken your first step toward finding a college, and it wasn't painful at all. You have made a list of items about which you have strong feelings. You are identifying the difference between information you need and don't need.

Of course, they're not the only items you'll consider. Others just as important will come later. Every campus has its own personality and you'll eventually want to learn if your personalities mesh or clash. But your list is a start. It's a screen to eliminate all those colleges that don't meet one of your criteria. You have begun to narrow the field.

WHAT'S MISSING?

You may have noticed that a couple of items some people consider in selecting a college aren't recommended for your list. They are prestige and national rankings. Both reflect other people's opinions, which won't necessarily agree with yours.

If you truly want to find the schools that fit you best for four or more years of your life, you must make your own decisions based on your needs, your goals, your personality. Others' views make good reading but should not influence you.

If you are looking for a prestigious school just because of its prestige—if you want to go to Harvard so you can say you're at Harvard—you don't need this book. Apply to Harvard and see if you're accepted.

If, after serious consideration of all the factors involved, it turns out that Harvard is right for you, then, fine, go for it. I'll show you how as we stroll through the process. But it could be that a better fit, the place you'll thrive as a student, is Ohio Dominican or Frostburg State. You must decide.

This book is here to help.

Listen to Avik Roy. As a high school student in San Antonio, he earned a place on *USA TODAY*'s All-USA Academic First Team that annually honors the nation's outstanding students. He desperately wanted to go to MIT, and he made it. A year later, he told a *USA TODAY* reporter: "I was very concerned about getting into MIT. Upon getting here, I realized it wasn't as big a deal as I thought. Having MIT behind my name is not going to make or break my life."

If you want to find the schools that fit you best, make decisions based on your needs—not someone else's.

THE RANKINGS GAME

Rankings of colleges in national magazines are fun to read and excellent publicity for schools that rank high. They're not reasons for students to select one college over another.

The rankings reflect arbitrary criteria selected by the magazines' editors that won't necessarily be the criteria you would use in making a choice. The percentage of tenured faculty teaching freshman classes is a good statistic to have. So is the total number of books in a college library. Both are used in magazine rankings. But would you give those numbers the same weight the editors do? Would you consider other factors the editors don't?

A fine guidance counselor at a high school that annually sends graduates to Ivy League colleges considers the rankings a curse. As she puts it: "Just as I have convinced Susie, and Susie's mother, that College X is the proper place for Susie academically and socially, a list will appear ranking Colleges A, B, Y, and Z above College X. All my work is down the drain."

A more compelling reason for ignoring rankings is the shaky reliability of the statistics used to compile them. That's why *USA TODAY* no longer publishes a Choosiest College list, once an annual feature.

The Choosiest College list tried to rank colleges by how tough it is to get in. To make the list, a school had to accept fewer than 50 percent of the students who applied and enroll a freshman class with an SAT average above 1200. Eventually, *USA TODAY* learned that schools compile SAT averages in many ways. Some use all enrolled students. Some use all students except athletes. Some use all students who are accepted, whether or not they show up.

We were comparing apples and raisins.

Rankings in magazines are fun to read, but they're not reasons to select one college over another.

We also learned, from a member of a college board of trustees, that officials of the college were "adjusting" the numbers they submitted to major directories so they would be sure to make our list. Bam! We ended the Choosiest College list.

But *USA TODAY* wasn't quitting the rankings game. Not long thereafter, we gathered twenty of the best minds in higher education around a conference table to see if they could agree on a legitimate way to measure a college's selectivity. They could not. Thoughtful suggestions offered by some were just as thoughtfully carved up and discarded by others.

The dean of admissions at a prestigious Eastern university told us, in a moment of candor, that whatever criteria were selected, his school could manipulate its numbers to make itself look good. *USA TODAY* quit the game.

THE MOST EXPENSIVE

Barnard now is the most expensive college in the country, charging $26,770 for tuition, room and board. But 45 schools had bills over $25,000 for the 1994–95 school year. (Books and transportation will add more to the cost.)

College	Cost
Barnard College, New York, NY	$26,770
Brandeis University, Waltham, MA	26,580
Yale University, New Haven, CT	26,350
Sarah Lawrence College, Bronxville, NY	26,258
Tufts University, Medford, MA	26,172
Hampshire College, Amherst, MA	26,145
University of Pennsylvania, Philadelphia, PA	26,126
Massachusetts Institute of Technology, Cambridge, MA	26,075
Bard College, Annandale-on-Hudson, NY	26,025
New York University, New York, NY	26,001
Brown University, Providence, RI	25,954
Middlebury College, Middlebury, VT	25,920
Swarthmore College, Swarthmore, PA	25,900
Princeton University, Princeton, NJ	25,810
Bennington College, Bennington, VT	25,800
Columbia College, New York, NY	25,732
Dartmouth College, Hanover, NH	25,719
Oberlin College, Oberlin, OH	25,616
University of Chicago, Chicago, IL	25,616
Johns Hopkins University, Baltimore, MD	25,600

continued

As I said, rankings are fun to read. Take them with a grain of salt. And don't put them on your list.

MAYBE YOU'RE NOT A KID

Adult students should start the process with the same list as their younger brethren. All the items—distance, size, location, majors—are relevant to all students regardless of age. Think about what's important to you.

THE MOST EXPENSIVE—continued

College	Cost
Reed College, Portland, OR	25,600
Harvard University, Cambridge, MA	25,596
Boston University, Boston, MA	25,580
Williams College, Williamstown, MA	25,561
Tulane University, New Orleans, LA	25,500
Bryn Mawr College, Bryn Mawr, PA	25,475
Stanford University, Stanford, CA	25,465
Colby College, Waterville, ME	25,420
Smith College, Northampton, MA	25,373
Amherst College, Amherst, MA	25,352
Hobart College, Geneva, NY	25,321
William Smith College, Geneva, NY	25,321
Cornell University, Ithaca, NY	25,304
Connecticut College, New London, CT	25,250
Haverford College, Haverford, PA	25,250
Trinity College, Hartford, CT	25,250
Bowdoin College, Brunswick, ME	25,240
Bates College, Lewiston, ME	25,180
Vassar College, Poughkeepsie, NY	25,170
Mount Holyoke College, South Hadley, MA	25,135
Union College, Schenectady, NY	25,126
Pomona College, Claremont, CA	25,120
Pepperdine University, Malibu, CA	25,040
Wesleyan University, Middletown, CT	25,040
Pitzer College, Claremont, CA	25,032

Source: Peterson's Guides, Inc.

Be reassured that, regardless of your age, most colleges want you. Older students often have an edge getting into college because of the diversity in outlook, maturity, and life experience they bring to the class. And today's economic reality, where the pool of high school graduates is smaller than the number of spots in freshman classes, means many colleges need older students to stay solvent.

An additional consideration for older folks who haven't been in a classroom for years is the two-year option.

Be reassured that, regardless of your age, most colleges want you. Older students often have an edge.

If you're a little scared about returning to school, not sure you're still able to cope with academic work, think about starting with a class or two at a local community college. You can build a record with credits that will transfer to a four-year college. And a good record at a community college will outweigh any academic lapses that may appear on your high school transcript.

Two-year colleges, of course, are options for all students. I talk more about them in Chapter Ten.

CHAPTER TWO

FINDING A FIT

. . . a no-stress route to a short list of "right" colleges

Your choices are vast. Colleges of all sizes, shapes, personalities, and degrees of academic challenge are out there offering you an education in exchange for your tuition dollars. Some are actively trying to persuade you that you'll love their beautiful campuses. And no two are identical.

The task of finding a few schools where you could thrive as a student—the short list to which you'll apply—can seem confusing, overwhelming, even traumatic. The key to avoiding this trauma is to take it one step at a time. Each step in the process is an easy one.

The process, and this chapter, are called "Finding a Fit," because that's exactly what you'll be doing. As you would try on suits, dresses, or gloves until you find some that fit comfortably, you will be trying on colleges.

Armed with your list of important items and other factors that have not yet entered your mind, you will gradually narrow the field of 3,200 accredited colleges to 4 or 5, maybe 6, where you could be successful and happy. You will become a consumer deciding what could be the most important purchase of your life.

WHAT YOU'RE NOT DOING

At this point, you're not looking for one single "right" college. There probably is no such thing. You'll find several campuses that will be right for you, probably in slightly different ways. From them, you'll select a first choice and hope that you'll be accepted. But just in case you're not, or in case you can't afford your first choice because it doesn't offer enough aid, you'll have other choices with which you'll be just as comfortable.

And you won't be picking a school because someone else likes it. Welcome and listen to all the advice you can get, particularly from parents, counselors, teachers you respect, and friends who have gone through the process. But the decision must be yours. It's your life that is being shaped. It is you who will fail or succeed. It's you who must make the fit.

> **The key to avoiding the trauma of selecting colleges is to take it one step at a time.**

Dad may want you to go to Yale because he's a Yale man. And you may have an edge getting into Yale because Dad went there, especially if he is a generous alumnus. If, after investigating Yale, you find it doesn't fit you, advise Dad as politely and firmly as you can that Yale is off your list.

If it will help, I'll give him the same advice right now: Back off, Dad. Sing the praises of Yale as loud as you'd like, but when your daughter decides Yale doesn't fit her, don't push it. You'd be hurting her more than helping.

THE KEY QUESTION

You have your list of important items. Now there's one more thing you must do to start your search. Ask yourself the key question: Why do I want to go to college? And answer it, to yourself, truthfully.

Do you want to go to college because your friends are going? Because your parents expect it? Because you'll make more money with a degree? Because you want to prepare yourself for a career? Because you won't know as much as you think you should know after high school? Because it's an easy way to cut the ties to your parents' nest? Because you can't think of anything else to do?

Your answer may be some, or all, of the above. It undoubtedly will change as you continue to ask the question through your high school years. The answer could help find your fit.

THE IDEALS

The ideal time to start looking for a fit is in eighth grade. A head start in thinking about it will stretch out the process and make the later steps flow easier.

If eighth grade is in your past, don't worry. Regardless of when you start, you can crunch it all in. But the earlier you begin, the more relaxed you can be. The timetable here is based on the ideal.

Ask yourself: Why do I want to go to college? And answer it truthfully.

If you're starting in eleventh grade, you'll spend more of your junior year doing it but you can still get it done.

The numbers in the examples below also are based on ideals. But they won't necessarily be the right numbers for you. The example starts with a list of 74 colleges and eventually picks 11 to visit. Your numbers, in both cases, could be higher or lower and still be right. The numbers here merely illustrate the process.

THE PRELIMINARIES: GRADES 8-9

As an eighth grader, take some time now and then to think about what interests you. Four years from now, when you're about to leave high school, are there fields in which you'd like to be involved?

Perhaps you already have a music talent? Or you enjoy math-related work? These thoughts will help you to be ready for the first decision that will affect your college life.

In the spring of eighth grade, you'll talk to a counselor about the courses you'll take next year. That's your first college-bound decision. The record you compile from ninth grade on is the record colleges look at.

Discuss with the counselor the activities and interests about which you've been thinking. Talk about courses you could take to see if those interests are real. You also should be talking about courses that will make you a strong college candidate. We'll explore that more thoroughly in Chapter Five.

In ninth grade, while you're earning grades that eventually will impress a college admission office, spend a day or two visiting a nearby college. Walk around the campus to get a feel for it. Stroll through the library and student center. Read bulletin boards. If you get a chance, talk to people. You'll begin to form an idea of what a college feels like.

A head start will stretch out the process and make the later steps flow easier.

If you have more than one college in your area, check out all of them. You will begin to see the difference between large and small, public and private, two-year and four-year colleges.

If possible, find a college student to visit: an older sibling, a cousin, a friend of the family. Spend some time in her dorm room to get the feel of the place.

THE START: GRADE 10

Make the list described in Chapter One. It will tell you the significance, in your own mind, of the basic variables that make colleges different from each other: size, location, distance from home, majors, academic rigor, housing, types of students, and cost.

YOUR FIT-FINDING TIMETABLE

8th Grade

Think about what you might want to study in college. Plan a high school schedule to best prepare for it.

9th Grade

Visit a local college and stroll around the campus to get a feel for it. If you know someone living in a dorm, make a visit.

10th Grade

Make a list of important factors (size, location, etc.) and decide how important each is.

Make a list of colleges that meet your most important factors.

Take the PSAT.

Read all the unsolicited mail from colleges. You may find something you like.

Visit a college fair; talk to representatives of colleges that appeal to you.

11th Grade Fall

Narrow down your list of colleges based on what you've learned since tenth grade.

Write for information from colleges still on your list.

Talk to friends, teachers, and alumni about colleges still on your list.

Visit a college fair again; you might find a college to add to your list.

Take the PSAT a second time for your shot at a National Merit Scholarship.

11th Grade Spring

Take the SAT and/or ACT.

Make your final cut to a short list of colleges to visit.

Schedule campus visits for now or next fall.

12th Grade Fall

Take SAT II Subject Tests as you finish specific courses.

Visit campuses you didn't get to in the spring.

Decide on three to six schools to which you'll apply.

Take SAT and/or ACT a second time, if you want.

Work on your application essay. Show it to an English teacher.

Line up a teacher and a counselor to write letters of recommendation.

Submit Financial Aid PROFILE if colleges request one.

12th Grade December

Fill out and submit applications.

Fill out FAFSA (Free Application for Federal Student Aid)

12th Grade January 2

Mail financial aid application.

Weigh each of the items by their importance. Use a scale of 1 to 5 or A to E or something similar to give yourself a written record of how much importance you're putting on each.

If you have strong specific feelings in any category, write down those specifics. For example, if you live in the East and want to stay there, write "East" after location. If you want to limit your search to certain states, write them. If you know you want a smaller campus, write "under 5,000" after size.

Don't be too restrictive with specifics because you'll be unnecessarily ruling out schools you might like.

The First Cut

This will take a little work. Your high school counseling center or school library should have some thick directories offering statistical profiles of all accredited colleges. If your school doesn't have them, your public library and local bookstore will.

In ninth grade, visit a nearby college. Walk around the campus to get a feel for it.

The profiles will tell you how close each college comes to the criteria on your list: its size, location, majors, SAT/ACT averages, number of students in dorms, etc. They also contain a lot of other statistics that you may or may not find interesting.

Hey, stop sweating! Just because those directories have 2,000 pages doesn't mean you have to read every one. They make it easy on you. After all, you're the customer.

Most directories list colleges alphabetically by state. All in Alabama come first, then Alaska, etc. If you have an idea where you want to go to college, or have identified a part of the country for your search, just check those states.

The better directories also have separate lists of schools meeting certain criteria. They'll give you all colleges in various size ranges, all with urban, suburban, or small-town campuses, all that offer majors in agriculture (or whatever).

Now it's time to make a second list. It can be as long as you would like. It should contain names of colleges that meet your most important priorities.

Let's say, for example, you've decided you definitely want a small to medium-sized four-year college and you want it to be in Michigan, Ohio, or Indiana. Other factors, at this point, aren't so important.

Go to a directory's lists and look for colleges with fewer than 5,000 students in those three states. You'll find 97. You can immediately tell by their names that 23 are specialized colleges— seminaries, art institutes, business or nursing schools, the Cincinnati College of Mortuary Science. Those fields don't interest you, so strike them. That leaves 74—a fine number with which to start.

On your list, write the names of the 74 colleges and their states. Then go to the main section of the directory and read their profiles. Note on your list next to each school's name other information that is important to you. (Remember, that total of 74 is being used to illustrate the process. Your number could be much lower or much higher, depending on your priorities.)

The directory profiles will tell you how close each college comes to the criteria on your list.

As you read, you could learn something that removes a school from your list. You may have decided, perhaps, that you're not that interested in big-city colleges. You find 9 with urban campuses. Delete them. That leaves 65.

You find 6 more that have no on-campus residences. All their students commute. You're looking forward to campus life as part of your college experience. Cross out those 6. The list is down to 59.

This task will take a few hours, maybe half a day. It's a valuable way to spend half a day in tenth grade. You now have identified 59 colleges—from the vast universe of 3,200— about which you'd like to know more. Put the list away for a while and get back to tenth-grade geometry.

Directories on Computer

You might be able to skip the directories and do the same work on your computer. At least three of the directory publishers offer software programs containing much of the same information found in their directories. They're priced out of a typical family's range but are often available to you through your high school or library. If either has purchased such a program the list could take less time than you thought. Such software can help you come up with a targeted list quickly; then you can go back to the books for more extensive information on the schools you're most interested in. As you choose your criteria—location, number of students, public or private, and so forth—the computer removes the schools that don't offer what you're looking for. The whole process could take as little as 20 minutes.

> **At least three of the directory publishers offer software programs containing the same information.**

Take the Test

A date to mark in big circles on your tenth-grade calendar is the autumn Saturday when you can take the PSAT. It's a good idea to take all the college-oriented tests that come your way. You invest a few hours, usually on a Saturday morning, for what could be significant dividends. One that should not be missed is the PSAT in tenth grade.

The PSAT's main role is preparation for its big brother, the SAT. Its scores are intended to give you an idea of your strengths and weaknesses as you prepare for the SAT in later years.

An equally important role, and one where potential dividends lie, is as a qualifier for the National Merit Scholarship Program. It's often identified as PSAT/NMSQT. The latter initials stand for National Merit Scholarship Qualifying Test.

The folks who run the National Merit Scholarships select semi-finalists solely on scores from the PSAT taken in eleventh grade.

Taking it in other years doesn't count. But taking it in tenth grade gives you an idea of what it's like and makes you more comfortable when you confront it again a year later.

Here Comes the Mail

By the time tenth grade ends, you may be tired of seeing your mail carrier. If you're a good student you will receive dozens, maybe hundreds, of letters from colleges, accompanied by brochures, fliers, and assorted other literature. They'll use pretty pictures and flowery adjectives to persuade you to give them four years of your life and your tuition dollars. You are being recruited.

How did they get your name? They bought it. For about 15 cents.

When you took the PSAT, you filled out a form providing demographic data about yourself. That information, along with your PSAT score, goes into a database maintained by the College Board, the organization that owns the SAT and PSAT. Colleges buy mailing lists of students whose scores are in a certain range, who fit a certain demographic profile, and who gave their approval on the PSAT form to release such information about themselves.

The PSAT's main role is preparation for its big brother, the SAT.

Andrew Dubill of Alexandria, Virginia, son of *USA TODAY*'s executive editor, collected two large trash bags full of unsolicited recruiting literature during his sophomore and junior years. And that's just what came after he started saving it for curious *USA TODAY* reporters.

Despite the hassle of opening all that mail, welcome it as a sign that colleges are interested in you. It gives you an idea of the type of college to which you can apply with a reasonable shot at being accepted.

"The more mail you get, the more you are in demand," says Andrew Weller, admission officer at Marymount University in Virginia. "We only buy those people who fit what we want."

Some of the mailings may be helpful. They might come from some of the 59 schools on your preliminary list. Chances are good that colleges in Michigan, Ohio, and Indiana bought names of students from their own and neighboring states. Read those carefully. They may tell you something that moves the college higher on your list or makes you drop it. File those recruiting brochures in the same place you filed your list.

Check out all the other literature, too. Resist the temptation to toss it away unopened. Just by glancing at the pretty pictures and scanning the words alongside them, something might grab your attention and make you want to know more. File those, also. Then toss the rest.

Almost all colleges enclose with their mailings a card or coupon that you can return if you want to know more. If you don't reply, you're off their lists. It's up to you.

That college mail gives you an idea of the type of college to which you can apply with a reasonable shot at being accepted.

Some of the mailings could give you a laugh. Vassar College sent Andrew Dubill a brochure and suggested he read it "while you watch David Letterman." It was a clue that Vassar likes students who read and watch TV at the same time. The University of Chicago told Dubill that "your name and address are in our computer." But its computer didn't share the information because the letter was addressed, "Dear Student."

Go to a Fair

Colleges spend money to buy mailing lists because college is a buyers' market. The number of high school graduates each year is less than the number of places in freshman classes. That's why older students are eagerly welcomed. That's why you, the consumer, are in demand.

And that's why they have college fairs, events where colleges looking for students and students looking for colleges can meet each other. You might think of them as a higher education dating service. The fairs put you together. It's up to you and the college to find romance.

Fairs also come in many sizes. The simplest and most prevalent are "college nights" sponsored by a high school or group of schools. Colleges in the area send representatives to talk to, and answer questions from, students and parents. Colleges outside the area often have networks of alumni who represent them at high school college nights. Alumni, as a rule, are less informed about what's happening at their alma maters than people who work on the campus.

More grandiose are national and regional fairs organized by the National Association of College Admission Counselors and its regional affiliates. They have booths set up by 150 or more colleges from across the country. Students have been known to arrive on convoys of yellow buses, organized by counseling offices, that have traveled 100 miles or more. These fairs usually are in convention centers or large hotels in major cities. High schools within a couple hours' drive are notified well in advance.

> **A conversation with an admission officer could give you vibes about whether the school should stay on your list.**

Sometime during tenth grade, go to a fair even if it's just a local college night. It will be your first chance to talk in person with college officials who want to talk with you.

Ask about anything that interests or puzzles you. If you are leaning toward certain majors, ask about those departments. If you're wondering about dorm life or the academic criteria for admission or the quality of the marching band, ask. Those folks' only job that night is to provide answers.

If some of the 59 colleges on your list are at the fair, so much the better. A conversation with an admission officer could give you some vibes about whether the school should stay on your list.

Meanwhile, check your counseling center regularly for brochures sent by schools on your list and any others that catch your eye. This is a time to collect information that will help you start making decisions next year.

THE MIDDLE: GRADE 11

You're halfway through high school. You have an academic record for two years that will impress some admission officers. You're committed to a couple of school activities. You've thought seriously, from time to time, about why you want to go to college and what you'd like to do when you get there. It's time to take out that list of colleges and cut it again. And perhaps add a name or two.

Since you made the list several months ago, you've talked to many people, read many brochures, focused your thoughts a little more clearly. You decided, after taking a walk around a very small campus in the next town, that very small is not for you. You'd like a wider mix of students and activities than you'll get at the tiniest colleges.

> It's time to take out that list of colleges and cut it again. And perhaps add a name or two.

For your preliminary list, you looked at colleges with fewer than 5000 students. Now you'd like to forget anything smaller than 1,000.

You're also getting a feel for what you might like to study in college. Let's say you found that you really like science classes. You enjoy tinkering in the biology lab, even stay after school to do so. But you're not sure your interest is strong enough to make science a career.

You learned, from your job at a day camp last summer, that you enjoy working with younger kids. You're delighted when you can show them how something works and see the lights snap on in their minds. Just maybe, you think, you might like to be a science teacher. At least your feelings are stronger in that direction than anywhere else.

So you wonder. At college would you major in education and take a little science on the side? Or would you concentrate on science with enough education courses to get a teaching certificate? Stop wondering. That decision can come later after you have enough information to make it wisely.

For now, go back to your list. It's shorter than it used to be. From talking to friends and people you worked with last summer, you've heard that 2 of the colleges are big into fraternities and sororities—that party life dominates their campuses. That's not your style. You've scratched those 2. You drew a line through another name after reading about a burglary in one of its dorms. With those 3 schools gone, your list is down to 56.

In the notes on your list, made from the school profiles in the directory, you see that 21 of the colleges have enrollments of under 1,000. Now that you've decided those schools are too small for you, their names go. You're left with 35.

The notes remind you that 3 colleges have single-sex student bodies. A single-sex campus once had some appeal but, a year later, you decide you'd like a balanced male/female student mix. Three more names off. Down to 32.

Attached to your list is a business card from an admission counselor at the University of Dayton. You met him at a fair last spring, liked what he had to say, and saved his card as a reminder to learn more. But Dayton isn't on your list because its 6,000 students put it outside your size range. You add it.

And you've heard a lot of good things about the University of Michigan—its academic and social life—from friends who go there. It has 22,000-plus students, a giant campus you'd like to avoid, but you're not ready to rule it out. Michigan goes on your list. Back up to 34.

Now it's time to return to the counseling center or library (or a computer) and pull out that directory. You want to know how many of those 34 colleges offer majors in science and education. You could learn that in the directory's list of majors. But just to see what you might have missed the first time, you check all 34 college profiles.

You learn that 27 of the 34 have majors in the two areas to which you're leaning. Scanning the profiles, you find one that indicates religion plays a dominant role in campus life. You're a religious person but the religion that pervades the campus doesn't happen to be yours. You don't think you could thrive in that environment. Down to 26.

In just a couple of hours, you have trimmed your list of colleges by more than half: from 55 to 26. You can call them your 26 semifinalists.

As it turns out, 12 of the 26 are in Ohio, 9 in Michigan, 5 in Indiana. Three are public colleges, the rest private. Their costs for tuition, room and board range from $6,693 to $21,180, and that's counting the higher out-of-state tuition at a public college. (Again a reminder. The numbers used here are for illustration. Yours will be different.)

You have trimmed your list of colleges by more than half; these are your semifinalists.

Writing Time

Now you're getting serious. Your next step, still early in eleventh grade, is writing to the admission offices at the 26 colleges asking for all the information they care to send about their institutions. Tell them of your interests, that you're leaning toward majoring in science or education. Mention the talents you have developed, such as playing trombone in the band and writing for your school newspaper.

You won't really write 26 letters. You'll write just one on your computer and give it 26 different addresses. Some of the college selection programs even help you do that; they've got the college addresses already available in their software.

While you wait for the return mail, work on that "A" in eleventh-grade chemistry.

Open the Other Mail

And while you wait, the unsolicited mail will still come. If something arrives from one of the 26 schools on your list, read it and file

A TYPICAL INFORMATION REQUEST

Here is a sample letter requesting information from colleges on your list. Names and addresses can be obtained from most college directories.

Peter J. Pickie
Dean of Admissions
1111 Main Hall
Nearby State University
Nexttown, OH 44444

Dear Dean Pickie:

I am a junior at Central High School in Niceville, Ohio, seeking information on colleges that might fit my needs after graduation. Because Nearby State offers majors in science and education, it is on my list of colleges under consideration.

Please send me all relevant information on your requirements for admission, courses available, campus housing, and financial aid. Please also include anything else you might like me to know about Nearby State that will help me make an informed decision.

Sincerely,
Sara Student

it. It says that that school is interested in you. You'll want to consider it with everything else you get. Otherwise, just glance at the stuff to see if anything piques your interest.

The Search Services

Also arriving in the mail will be ads from companies offering to help you—for a fee, of course—with your search. Some will promise to find you scholarships. (I'll talk about those in Chapter Eight when we look at sources of money.) Others are selling videos or CD-ROMs that give you a close-up, full-color look at college campuses without the hassle of visiting them.

Should you buy them? That's up to you and your parents, if they pay the bill. But there are two things to consider. The videos and computer disks contain information only on colleges that have paid to be there, usually a small fraction of all the colleges in the country.

And the presentations are developed by the colleges to show themselves in the best light. They are electronic versions of the brochures
and viewbooks you can get free from the college itself.

Take the tests

Yes, take the tests. Take all that you can: the PSAT, the SAT 1,
SAT II Subject Tests, the ACT. None by itself is a key to getting into
college, but all can help.

SAT SCORES BY COLLEGE MAJOR

Students taking the SAT are asked their expected college major. Potential
math majors score highest, home economists lowest. Here are 1994 SAT
average scores by major.

Math	1082
English, literature	1047
Engineering	999
Philosophy, religion	987
Biological science	983
Foreign language	981
Physical science	970
Library science	938
Social science	929
Communications	906
Military science	905
Undecided	905
ALL STUDENTS	902
Architecture	899
Arts	897
Computer science	894
Health services	891
Business	866
Agriculture	863
Education	854
Public affairs	791
Home economics	788

Source: The College Board

A crucial test is the PSAT in the fall, usually October, of eleventh grade. That's the test whose score can qualify you as a National Merit Semifinalist.

National Merit Semifinalists find doors flung open to them in college admission and financial aid offices. If you eventually become a National Merit Finalist, your college application leaps to the top of many admission office stacks. At colleges where enrolling merit scholars is a high priority, all else about you will be secondary.

You can't become a merit finalist unless you're a semifinalist. You can't be a semifinalist unless you take the PSAT in eleventh grade. That's a fact of student life.

Sad tales abound from college students who have the talent to be merit scholars but did not earn that honor because no one told them to take the PSAT in eleventh grade. More about this in Chapter Eight, where we'll find ways to locate college money.

Take the SAT/ACT also in spring of eleventh grade. If you like your score, fine. That hurdle is passed. But if you think you could do better, plan to take it again next spring in twelfth grade. Then

> **Take the PSAT as practice for the SAT— and hopefully to qualify you as a National Merit Semifinalist**

perhaps a third time next fall. It can only help, not hurt. Each time you take it, you'll be more familiar and more comfortable with it. And on a national average, a student's score increases 40 points each time he retakes the SAT.

Almost all colleges now look only at your highest score regardless of how many times you take the test. I'll talk about the tests' role in the admission process in Chapter Four.

One More Cut

The eleventh-grade chemistry class is tough but fun. You're enjoying it just as much as biology. You are becoming convinced you would like to pursue college-level science. But you're not sure which science.

In your second summer at day camp, you also became convinced that you have a talent for making kids understand things. And you like the challenge. You're focusing hard on the idea of life as a science teacher.

You talk to your counselor and to some of your teachers seeking advice. Your chemistry teacher, whose wisdom you respect, says you should study as much science as possible and fill in with the education courses necessary to learn the teaching ropes.

Others advise you to wait until you've tasted the full menu of high school science courses to decide which interests you most.

They suggest you hold off even until you get to college before declaring a specific major. You're luckier than many eleventh graders. You're getting good advice.

The next cut will leave the colleges about which you're serious enough to go for a "personality" check.

As the mail you've requested from 26 colleges begins to arrive, you're now reading it as a student who wants to major in science and minor in education.

You've been making subjective decisions rooted in facts for more than a year. Now the process becomes even more subjective. Based on what you read in the piles of literature from the 26 colleges and what you've learned elsewhere, you must narrow the list once more.

The next cut will leave only the colleges about which you're serious enough to go for a "personality" check.

It's going to be easy. You already have 5 or 6 emotional favorites—schools that for one reason or another hit a responsive chord as you learned about them. As you read catalogs, 2 colleges' descriptions of their science curriculums make excellent impressions.

Then there's that school in Ohio where, because you expressed an interest in science, the chemistry department chair sent you a personal letter inviting you to visit. And what's this? A catalog from a Michigan college says it offers a major in science education.

You eliminate 12 colleges that have given you no reason to make them stand out. That leaves 14. You notice that 3 have enrollments around the 1,200 level, which is close to too small for your tastes. You're sure you won't be applying there.

Your list has 11 names remaining—11 colleges at which you think you can be happy, have a full social life, and learn to be a science teacher. You think you can but you're not sure. You know, however, which colleges you want to try on to see if you have a fit.

It's time for the final test. The personality check. Every college has its own distinct personality just as you have yours. Before you start filling out applications, you must know if your personalities mesh or clash. The only way to find out is to go there.

You've now been through the start and the middle of the process. You started with a book full of 3,200 colleges and you have 11 finalists. It's spring of eleventh grade.

And this chapter now ends because the final stage—the six months between now and next October—is so important it deserves a chapter by itself. It's when you visit 11 campuses. When you come home from the last of them, you'll be certain that you have found colleges that fit you nicely. Then you will apply.

Again, a reminder. There's nothing magic about the number 11. It's the number used to illustrate the process of narrowing your choices. Your list of schools to visit could have fewer than 11 names or many more. Some students have visited 25 and 30 campuses, some 5 and 6.

MAYBE YOU'RE NOT A KID

Adults looking at college usually are into the fit-finding process when the looking begins. If you're over 25, thinking seriously about entering or returning to college, you already know why.

You have, whether you realize it or not, a focus—a goal that college will help you reach. You likely already have decided what you want to study to reach that goal. You have identified colleges that offer the program you desire.

If you want to continue to work and attend college, you're restricted to schools within a short drive of home. Because of that and other factors, you have a short list already in your mind. A likely one is a two-year community college in your hometown, an increasingly popular reentry avenue for college-bound adults. (See Chapter Ten.)

It still won't hurt to check one of those big college directories. Read about the schools you are considering. Perhaps look at others in your area that you hadn't thought about to see if they have anything to offer you. Check out the colleges' "adult friendliness."

Check out the colleges' "adult friendliness"; do they have night courses and weekend programs, adult student advisers?

Do they have a wide range of night courses and weekend programs of interest to you? Do they have advisers specifically for adult students? It won't cost anything but a couple hours.

With a short list of colleges in hand, maybe containing just one or two names, it would be beneficial for you, even more so than for teenagers, to visit their campuses for a personality check.

Can you thrive as a student at College A, B, or C? The only way to answer with any certainty is to go there and find out.

And that's where we go next.

CHAPTER THREE

THE PERSONALITY CHECK

. . . have one date before you get engaged

Would you marry someone you've never met? Well, you're about to make a commitment to spend four years of your life with a group of people you don't even know. It's a good idea to meet some of them first. Indeed, it's an essential step to find the colleges that truly fit you.

We all learn early in life that some people, and some things, are different than they first seem. People we would like to know turn out to be jerks. Others we at first avoid wind up close friends.

The same can be true with colleges. A campus that has enthralled you with its literature and its letters could, on closer inspection, have a personality that sharply conflicts with yours. The only way to learn its personality is by visiting its campus.

The concept of a college having a personality was not invented for this book. The term is used widely by students after meeting colleges up close. Brian Caveney, a *USA TODAY* academic all-star who turned down Ivy League offers to stay home at West Virginia University, says: "Every university has its own personality that's de-termined by the size, the student body, and the administration. This university really fit my personality."

The son and daughter of *USA TODAY* editors, now attending their second colleges, left their first choices after one year because of severe personality clashes. One chose a high-prestige university because it was considered a plum among her high school peers. She enrolled without checking its personality. She was miserable. The other picked a small liberal arts college in a tiny eastern town far from any large city. He quickly learned that his personality was not meshing and the campus isolation increased his frustration. He trans-ferred to a large public university in his home state where he's thriving.

"Every university has its own personality that's determined by the size, the student body, and the administration."

A more satisfying experience is re-ported by *USA TODAY* editor Anita Manning and her daughter, Katie Barras. Katie was considering several colleges and chose Smith after an overnight visit to its Massachusetts campus.

"The visit sold her," says her mother. "She liked the intellectual challenge it seemed to offer, the small classes, and she was comfortable with the students." After two years, Katie's first impressions haven't changed.

Now with your short list of 11 colleges, or whatever your number happens to be, it's time to see how your personality fits. It's time to plan campus visits.

THE ESSENTIALS

Each campus visit will encompass many activities, giving you many opportunities to learn how the school functions. Each campus will differ in details depending on the school, the time of year you visit, and the time you have to spend.

But each visit should include four essential components:

1. An interview with a college admission officer. It gives you a chance to ask a person trained to deal with potential applicants the questions that the catalogs and viewbooks don't answer. And it gives the admission office a face and personality to go with the application you might send in later.

2. Informal talks with students, wherever you can find them. College students are among the most candid people on the planet. They'll be quick to offer their opinions on what's right and wrong with their school. And the more you talk, the better feel you get for the type of students at the college.

3. An overnight stay, in a dorm or in a nearby motel. You don't get a full, valid impression of a town, a community, or a college until you wake up there and have breakfast. A quickie, hurry-up, talk-to-a-few-people-and-leave visit is hardly any visit at all.

College students will be quick to offer their opinions on what's right and wrong with their school.

4. If you plan to apply for financial aid, a fourth essential should be a visit to the college financial aid offices. It serves the same purpose as the interview with the admission officer. You can ask specific questions and begin to build a rapport with someone who makes decisions about giving away money. If you volunteer some basic information about your finances—parents' annual income, ballpark estimate of their assets—a seasoned financial aid officer can give you an educated guess about your chances of getting help.

THE PREPARATION

The best time for you to schedule a series of college visits is the summer because school's out and all your academic and extracurricular pressures have temporarily faded away. But the worst time to visit a college for a personality check is also the summer. For the same reason. School's out. The campus is inhabited only by the few students and professors attending summer classes. Its personality won't be in full bloom.

Your visits should come between the time you compile your short list at the end of eleventh grade and the time you start filling out applications in the winter of twelfth grade. If summer is the only time available, do it then. Summer visits are better than no visits. But the ideal visiting seasons are when the colleges are in full swing with classes in session and students around: your eleventh grade spring (April, May) and twelfth grade fall (September, October).

To get the most from your visit, plan your schedule in advance and call for appointments. You want an interview at the admission office and with a financial aid officer (see Chapter Eight for more on meeting with someone in financial aid).

> **The ideal visiting seasons are when the colleges are in full swing with all classes in session and all students around.**

If you have decided on a major, you should also talk to a professor in that department. You'll make a better first impression on all three if you call and ask for some of their time.

If you show up on a campus unannounced, you might get an interview and you might not. And if you do, the interviewer may not be happy about it because you could be adding extra time to her already busy day. It's not the reaction you want to produce.

Pick a day on which you'd like to visit and call at least two weeks in advance. Call the admission office first because an interview there is most important to you. With two weeks' notice, an admission officer surely will be able to schedule some time for you. Then call the financial aid office and any faculty you might like to chat with and ask for interviews on the same day.

Meanwhile, learn all you can about the schools you'll be visiting. If you or your parents know some alumni in the area, talk to them

TIPS FOR CAMPUS VISIT

Plan ahead. Schedule appointments with the admission office, financial aid office, and at least one professor in a field of particular interest.

Talk to alumni in your area before the visit

Read all college literature ahead of time

Prepare a list of questions and things to check out while on campus

Take parents along, if possible

Stay overnight, preferably in a dorm

Talk to students wherever you can find them

Visit a class in progress

Read the campus newspaper; visit newspaper office to talk to staffers

Write thank-you notes when you get home

about their experiences. Write for some recent copies of the colleges' student newspapers. They'll bring you up to date on current campus issues.

SHOULD YOUR PARENTS GO ALONG?

In some families, whether they have two parents or one, it's a given. Mom and/or Dad and student do the college shopping as a group. In others, it's not so simple. Parents may not be able to get time off from work. The needs of younger siblings may require one parent—or the only parent—to stay home.

If it's possible, a campus visit should be a family outing. Basic arithmetic shows it will be more productive that way. Six eyes and ears see and hear more than two of each. But *you*, the student, should take the lead: "I'm here for my two o'clock interview . . ."—not Mom saying "*we* are here. . . ."

Back in a motel room after a day on campus, three experiences mingled together and three people expressing opinions can produce a clearer perception of a school's personality than one person trying to discern it alone. And it's always possible that Dad might have seen something you missed.

In a family visit, however, it's important for family harmony and mental health that both parents and student remember their roles.

The student is the buyer, the consumer. It's the student's life that is about to be shaped. The decision on what college to attend must be the student's. The student must decide if her personality meshes with the college. The parents' personalities, at this point, are irrelevant.

Parents are advisers. Their advice should be plentiful, should be welcome, and should be seriously considered. But when the bottom line is reached, parents must back off and let the student decide.

THE CAMPUS TOUR

Your first stop on your campus visit may well be a tour. They're ubiquitous on all campuses in spring and fall. Groups of prospective students are assembled in a meeting room, hear a brief talk about the glories of the college, then are introduced to a student who leads them on a tour of campus sights that the admission office wants them to see.

A campus visit should be a family outing; six eyes and ears see and hear more than two of each.

When you call ahead for an appointment, an admission officer may suggest you arrive in time for a tour. If it fits your schedule, do so. If it doesn't, don't worry about it.

Campus tours are harmless. They offer live views of scenes you already have seen in brochures and catalogs. The student escort is working for the admission office and is describing scenes in words written by the admission office. When you ask her a question, it's likely one to which the admission office has supplied an answer.

The student tour guide, though, can be helpful in starting you on the rest of your investigation. Ask her where students hang out and socialize in their spare time. Ask about a public cafeteria, say in the student union, where students eat. Ask the location of the student newspaper office. All can be fine sources of information.

THE FACULTY

If you have decided on a major and have an appointment with a professor in that field, don't leave right away after you talk with him. Ask if you can sit in on a class, even for 15 minutes or so. Most professors would welcome you. If the professor doesn't have a class immediately scheduled, he'll probably introduce you to a colleague who does.

Your request to attend a class accomplishes two things. It shows the professor you have a serious interest in his field. He might mention this to the admission office, which will help your application. And you get a chance to see how a class is conducted. It's another item in your personality check.

If you don't have a faculty appointment, drop into a classroom area anyway. Hang around afterward and ask some questions. Pick a field in which you know you'll be taking classes. Introduce yourself to a receptionist in a faculty office area and ask about the possibility of sitting in on a class. She might work something out for you.

> **Your request to attend a class shows you're interested and you get to see how it's conducted.**

THE STUDENTS

You'll get the most valid personality check from the students who might soon be your peers. Seek them out in the cafeteria, the library, a classroom, and anywhere else you might encounter them. You'll find that most have opinions about their school that they're eager to share. They'll tell you about the rigor of classes, the social life, the dorms, the activities.

Journalists, as a rule, are more opinionated and more outspoken than others in their communities. That's true, too, of student journalists. Drop into the student newspaper office to chat with some staff members. The chats could be enlightening.

Reading the campus paper also can give you insight into student life and issues of student concern.

From talking to students, you'll also get a good feel for the types of student on the campus and the student culture. Do students get much one-on-one contact with professors? Are computers a dominant item in student life? Are parties a high student priority? Is the prevailing dress style long-hair and grungy or clipped-short and neat? Are some majors considered tough and others snaps? Answers to these and many other questions define a college's personality.

And the bottom-line question for you: Do you feel this is a place where you can thrive academically and socially for four years?

THE OVERNIGHT STAY

The best way to learn about any group of people is living with them. Students are no exception. If you have a chance to spend a night in a college residence hall, grab it. Many colleges offer visiting students a night in a dorm. Some prefer you to ask in advance. When you call to set up an appointment, ask the admission office if a dorm stay is possible.

If the school doesn't offer you a dorm night, you'll have to find a student to give you a spare bunk or even a floor on which to spread a sleeping bag. If a friend from your high school or a distant cousin is attending the college, ask to spend the night in his room. You'll get a better fix on student life than anywhere else. If your parents are accompanying you, let them go to the motel. You sleep in the dorm.

If you can't find a dorm room, still plan to spend the night in the college town. Stroll the campus after dark. Check out the student union and library in the evening. If you've heard about a popular student gathering place, you might drop in there. In the morning, you'll have a fresh perspective on everything you've seen and heard.

If you have a chance to spend a night in a college residence hall, grab it.

WHEN YOU GET HOME

Yes, I know writing notes is a pain. But in this case, it can be worth the hassle. Within two days of your return home, get a note in the mail to everyone with whom you talked at length. Thank them for their time and help.

You didn't leave your campus visit in a vacuum. People do remember you. The admission officer with whom you talked for an hour, as we'll see in the next chapter, has notes about that conversation in her file. She also may have a note from the chemistry professor or music director you impressed. When your application arrives, she'll put those notes in your application folder.

Add your note to the collection. It need only be two or three sentences long. It will be read when it arrives and it will be read again when your application is considered. It will help create the impression you desire: that you are a thoughtful, considerate person who would be a welcome addition to a college student body.

Thank-you notes create the impression you would be a welcome addition to a college.

WHAT'S MISSING?

An important part of your campus visit was not discussed in detail here. It's your interview with a representative of the college admission office. It's important enough that it deserves a chapter of its own, which begins on the next page.

CHAPTER FOUR

THE INTERVIEW

. . . when you and the college each have something to learn

Some students fear it. They think it's more stressful than writing an essay or taking the SAT/ACT. They get moist palms just at the thought of presenting themselves in person to a sophisticated adult who could hold their future in his hands.

Students call *USA TODAY*'s College Admission Hotline each year seeking advice on how to get through the interview with minimal damage to their college chances. They're told, in effect, to relax and enjoy it. The interview is a two-way street. The college has as much to gain or lose from the conversation as the student.

If you're a good student with a good high school record, the college likely wants you as much as you want the college. Remember, it's a buyer's market. You're the buyer.

Here's one way to look at it. The admission officer interviewing you across a desk at College X will be, a few months later, the admission officer urging you to enroll in College X after you've been accepted by Colleges W, X, Y, and Z.

OK, now that your palms are dry, let's look at what an interview really is. It's a learning opportunity for both you and the college.

You want to learn if College X is a good fit. To make that decision, information from an admission officer is important. The college wants to learn if you are its kind of student. Talking to you helps it decide.

The admission officer will be more impressed with you if you come with a prepared agenda of information you want to obtain and you ask your questions confidently and politely. Dress casually for the interview and try to relax.

You'll undoubtedly be more impressed with the college if you feel the admission officer is sincerely trying to obtain information about you and not brushing you off as a nuisancc in a busy day.

So your goals and the college's goals are the same. Each of you wants to learn while informing. You want to see if you like the other party while trying to persuade the other party to like you.

Very few colleges these days *require* an interview as part of the admission process because they are reluctant to impose additional travel costs on potential students. Those that do, usually high-prestige, Ivy League–type schools, have **The interview is a two-way street; the college has as much to gain or lose as you do.** a network of alumni across the country trained to interview applicants in the student's hometown. These interviewers, typically self-employed professionals such as lawyers and architects, also are part-time employees or volunteers of the college admission office.

That said, all colleges welcome the opportunity to talk to students who visit their campuses. As I explained in Chapter Three, it's best to schedule an interview in advance. If you arrive unannounced you could find nobody home.

YOUR AGENDA

Your twin goals in the interview are to learn about the school and to inform the school about you. So you should be ready to talk about both subjects: the school and you.

Come prepared and ask questions confidently and politely.

Before you left home, you already had some questions about the college for which you couldn't find answers—and your parents probably had some of their own. You may be concerned about:

- The likelihood of getting all the courses you need to earn a degree in four years without getting shut out of some classes by overcrowding.
- The availability of on-campus living quarters as a freshman and in the years to come. And the types of off-campus residences for students who can't get into or don't want to be in the dorms.
- Security measures in the residence halls.
- How the faculty advising system works.
- What credit you'll get for your Advanced Placement high school courses.
- How much weight your SAT/ACT score gets in relation to the other items in your application.
- The chances of having real professors teach freshman courses instead of graduate-student teaching assistants.

Now is the time to ask those questions. If you don't receive adequate answers, that's something to consider when you decide if this college fits your needs.

But don't hurt yourself by asking the wrong questions. Don't show that you haven't read the literature you received. If the college viewbook clearly says 70 percent of freshmen live in dorms, don't ask what percentage of freshmen live in dorms. You'll be creating the impression that you don't really care enough to read about the college in advance. Ask instead about the chances of becoming part of that 70 percent who gets into the dorms.

When the conversation turns to you, offer some information about what you're doing in high school, the courses you're taking, and what you'd like to accomplish in college. If you have a special talent, like music or theater, mention it and explain why you like it. The admission officer may call someone in the music or drama department to set up an interview for you.

Tell the admission officer why you're interested in her college. Describe briefly the process you used to develop a short list of schools you're visiting. And be honest. Tell her that you haven't decided where to apply and this visit is to help you make that decision. Your honesty will be remembered favorably if you apply.

If you're the student who walked through the preliminary fit-finding steps in Chapter Two, tell the admission officer, for instance, about your interests in science and teaching and your desire to become a science teacher. Ask for her opinions on how to best achieve that goal at her college.

If you're prepared (and have read this book), you're also aware that some things on your high school record will raise questions when your application arrives in the admission office. You now can answer those questions before they arise.

Few schools *require* an interview these days.

If your grades were great in ninth and eleventh grades but took a tumble your sophomore year, explain why that happened. Perhaps your mother was hospitalized and your responsibilities for younger siblings hurt your school work. That could be a mitigating factor.

It's a good idea to bring a copy of your high school transcript. Some admission officers won't be interested in it but others will. And it's the only time you'll have a chance to discuss it with an admission officer face to face. If you received a B in biology from a teacher who rarely gives A's, that's information the admission officer should have and this is the time to convey it.

And don't be reluctant to ask about your prospects. An admission officer can tell you if your academic record is in the range of students usually admitted. If you're visiting in eleventh grade, don't be shy about asking how you can improve your transcript in your senior year.

TIPS FOR THE INTERVIEW

Ask About . . .

Admission requirements

Advanced Placement credits

Campus security

Chances of getting a degree in four years

Campus residential life

Use of graduate students to teach classes

Don't Ask About . . .

Things you should know from reading literature sent to you (read it carefully before the interview)

College Wants to Know . . .

Is your interest sincere

Are you capable of handling the work

Are you self-confident

Do you have a sense of humor

Do you speak well

Although you have not yet applied to the college, the admission officer should be taking notes for her file in case an application comes. If she isn't taking notes, it's a sign she's not really interested— another sign that this college may not be right for you.

THE COLLEGE'S AGENDA

The admission officer uses the interview to learn things about you that it won't find in your application. And since you haven't decided if you'll apply yet, she wants this opportunity to persuade you that her college is a good place for you.

Because it's a buyer's market (and I can't repeat that often enough), most colleges these days have customer-oriented admission staffs whose jobs are as much recruiting and marketing as deciding who gets in. In the interview, the admission officer wants to learn about you while promoting her college. But not all interviews are equal. The more attractive you appear as a student, the more she will use the interview as a recruiting tool.

> **Don't ask questions that are answered in the college's literature.**

The only schools at which recruiting is not a significant part of the admission office's work are those 35 or 40 who annually get the top-level high school students and receive three times as many applications as they need.

More important to you, of course, is how to come across as an attractive student. The admission officer will be listening not only to what you say but how you say it. Do you show a sincere interest in the college—or do you seem to be on a fishing trip? Do you seem self-reliant? Do you have a good self-image? Do you exude confidence? Do you show a sense of humor? Can you laugh easily? Do you articulate well—or speak in monosyllables and grunts? Those are among the questions in the mind of the admission officer as she sits down to talk with you. And as you talk, she looks for answers.

NOW WHAT?

After the interview, the ball is in your court. You will use the information you've obtained to help make your decision on which colleges fit best. You're now ready to decide which four, five, or six you'll favor with an application.

When you apply, the notes from your interview will be retrieved from an admission office file and attached with a paper clip to your application. It will go into a folder with your name on it. In a few days, that folder will be opened by an admission officer—very likely the same one with whom you talked. After about 15 minutes of reading, she'll give you a grade that will be a key in determining if the college wants you.

We'll discuss in Chapter Six the things you can do to make sure that grade is high. But first, it's decision time. Your shopping for a college has ended. You now must decide where you will apply.

CHAPTER FIVE

MAKING THE CHOICE

. . . when you stop browsing and pick

It's now early in your high school senior year, September or October. You've learned everything you can about 11 colleges. It's decision time.

By the time you got home from the last of your campus visits you had a good idea of the colleges to which you wanted to apply. You feel 3 schools—First U., Second College, and Third Tech—clearly stand out above the rest as places where you could thrive as a student and learn to be a science teacher. You were happy with what you heard from the faculty.

You built rapport with the students. The admission standards are in the range you could meet. Your personalities meshed. They are, in other words, good fits.

At each of the 3 colleges, financial aid officers were optimistic that you could get an aid package large enough to make the costs affordable.

Of the 3, you're definitely leaning toward First U. You found yourself very comfortable with all aspects of its campus, especially the night you spent in the dorm. If you had to pick just one, First U. would be it.

But First U., as well as Second College and Third Tech, are a bit selective about whom they admit. So just to be sure, you're ready to apply to all 3 colleges. At least one of them, you think, will want you as a student.

In the back of your mind, however, is Choosy U. You liked what you saw and heard. The chemistry prof was the most interesting faculty member you met at the 11 schools. You'd enjoy the challenge of taking his classes. It, too, is a good fit.

But Choosy U.'s admission requirements are pretty tough. Its freshmen average over 1300 on the SAT. Your score is 1230. It likes students in the top 10 percent of their high school classes. You're in the top 12 percent but not the top 10. It prefers three years of a foreign language in high school—you had two years of Spanish. You feel the chances of being accepted **It's September or October of your senior year—decision time.** at Choosy U. are low. It would be, in admission officers' jargon, a "reach" for you.

You think seriously about it. Perhaps you might get lucky. You could be one of those Choosy U. applicants who gets in for a reason you haven't even considered. (More about luck in Chapter Nine.) You talk to your high school counselor. She suggests that, while you're applying to your first three choices, you might as well give Choosy U. a shot. At this point, the only additional cost will be a couple hours of time and a 32-cent stamp. Again, you're unlike most high school seniors. You're getting good advice. Being a wise high school senior, you take it.

Now, as you're ready to pull out application forms and start writing, fear strikes. All 4 schools—First U., Second College, Third Tech, and Choosy U.—could say no. What then?

Suddenly another horrible thought: Suppose the financial aid officers are wrong. They warned you that their predictions of aid were just estimates and you wouldn't know for sure until after you submit a financial aid application. Maybe you can't afford to go to any of your top three choices.

You remember Nearby State, in a small city 2 hours away. It was on your list of 11 because it offers a nice combination of science and education courses and its 5,000 student enrollment is in your size range. You felt 100 percent certain you would be accepted at Nearby, and its in-state tuition is low enough that your parents could pay the tab without aid. You decide to add Nearby State as a fifth college to which you'll apply.

You're not alone. Almost every high school senior applying to college suffers the same panic attack and resolves it the same way. In admission officer jargon, you're applying to a "safe school," your "safety valve"—a school that you can live with and will be there in case all else fails.

Almost every senior applies to a "safe school," just in case all else fails.

It's time now to request your 15 minutes of attention at 5 college admission offices. We'll stroll together through that process in Chapter Seven. But first, let's pause to look at what the college wants to see when your application arrives.

CHAPTER SIX

WHAT COLLEGES WANT

. . . and how to convince them that they want you

You have found the right colleges. It took a long time, but you're happy with the 5 left on your list. Now comes the job of convincing each of those schools that you're the kind of student it would like to have on its campus.

The task should not be difficult. You're a high school senior. You have been building a record in academics, activities, and personal experiences for more than three years. All that remains to be done is to present that record to the colleges in an impressive package.

They already know you and think favorably about you from your campus visits. But they won't decide if you deserve one of the places in their freshman class until you tell them about yourself on an application.

The typical college application comes in many parts. One is a multipage form that asks for all kinds of facts about you. Other parts will be letters of recommendation from teachers and counselors. Some schools want you to write an essay. You will have to attach a list of your activities in school and the community. Then there's the all-important high school transcript.

Everything you've done since ninth grade will come through on your application.

Read the application from beginning to end before you start filling in anything or pulling together any information. It is not as intimidating as it appears. But by the time you put the application form on your desk and start answering questions, there is nothing you can do to change what it will say about you. Your record as a student and as a person has been compiled.

I've said it before and here it is again: The first person who reads your application package in a college admission office will spend 15 to 20 minutes on it. That's all the time you have to make an impression. The first impression, and the rating you get from that first admission officer, will go a long way in determining if you're accepted. The impression will be created in part by how your application looks but mainly by what it says.

WHAT YOUR APPLICATION SAYS

All parts of your application, taken together, will paint a portrait of your life as a high school student. Everything you have done since the start of ninth grade will come through.

So the ideal time to start preparing your application—to begin the record that will appear on the admission officer's desk—is before you get to high school. It's in eighth grade, when a counselor talks to you about courses you'll take the next year. The decisions you make during that conversation will appear on your high school transcript—the first piece of paper an admission officer picks up after she opens your envelope.

Dozens of other decisions you make during your high school years will be reflected on the papers (or electronic forms as we'll see in Chapter Seven) that you send to colleges. The courses you take, the clubs you join, the hobbies you pursue, the talents you develop, the jobs you hold, will be part of your record that's unchangeable when application time arrives.

HIGH SCHOOL COURSES

Is a "B" in a tough course worth more than an "A" in a snap?

It's a question heard regularly as each new class of high school students approaches its college application days. At *USA TODAY*'s College Admission Hotline, it comes up several times each year.

The answer never changes. It's a resounding "yes." The first item almost all colleges look at on an application is the list of courses on the transcript. Not the grades, but the list of courses. Your grade-point average (GPA) is important, but the path you took to get it tells more.

Colleges look first for evidence that you challenged yourself academically, that you prepared yourself for college work, that you don't run away from tough tasks. All this is learned from your high school course selection.

You may have been the nicest person the admission officer ever met during your campus visit. But if your school offers twelve Advanced Placement (AP) courses and you took none, your great

> **A "B" in a tough course is worth more than an "A" in a snap course.**

personality is instantly forgotten. Ask any admission dean at even a moderately selective college about factors in his decisions and he'll say something like: "First we look at what you've done. Then we look at how well you've done it."

In a 1994 survey by the National Association of College Admission Counselors (known as NACAC), 83 percent of the admission offices responding said grades in college-preparatory courses are "considerably important" in their admission decisions. Just one third said the same about grades in all courses.

Colleges look first at your record in the Big Five, the so-called "solid" subjects that make up the college-preparatory curriculum: English, math, science, social studies, and foreign language. Many would like to see four years of study in four of those areas and two years in foreign language. Most require a minimum number of solids as a condition for admission.

In all cases the more the better. If you have four years of English, math, and science, you score higher in a college admission office than your friend who has three years of each.

Then they look at what you've done in relation to what your high school offers. Are honors and AP courses available? If so, how many did you take? If you've challenged yourself with the toughest possible curriculum, you won't be penalized because your school offers nothing tougher.

Have you cluttered your high school years with easy courses— you know what they are—taken to get a sure "A" and pad your GPA? Unfortunately, that happens. The reaction it produces in admission offices is negative.

But where do you draw the line? If a "B" in an AP course is worth more than an "A" in a regular course, what about a "C" in the tougher course? The answer, frankly, depends on the school.

> **"First we look at what you've done. Then we look at how well you've done it."**

Gary Ripple of Lafayette College says: "If it's between a 'B' in an honors course and an 'A' in a regular course, the honors course wins every time. If it's a difference of one grade, you're better off in honors. If it's two grades, you're better off in the regular course."

At the University of North Carolina–Chapel Hill, one of the nation's most selective public colleges, Admission Director James Walters pulls the line down farther. "If a student can gain at least a 'C' in an advanced course," he says, "we would recommend every time that the student take the most challenging curriculum."

You learned how the 5 colleges on your short list weigh your grades when you talked to an admission officer during your campus visit. But that didn't help two years ago, when you were deciding which courses to take.

The best rule to follow: when in doubt opt for the toughest course. Regardless of where they draw the line, colleges will look more favorably on you for accepting a challenge than avoiding one.

CAN YOUR HIGH SCHOOL HURT YOU?

A myth is prevalent these days that colleges have a secret list ranking all high schools in the country and kids from the higher-ranked schools have the better shots. Parents calling *USA TODAY*'s 1994 College Admissions Hotline insisted they know where their schools rank on the list.

Let's bust the myth right now. No such list exists.

But yes, the admission office knows what your high school offers. It knows the strength of your school's curriculum compared to other schools in your region, even in your state. If you're in an area regularly served by the college, an admission officer has been assigned to know your school, know what various course titles mean, know the grading system, and know the full curriculum. She also has a computer printout showing how well graduates of your high school have done at her college. She's the expert on high schools in your area and probably will be the first to read your application.

> **The admission office knows the strength of your school's curriculum compared to other schools.**

Most high schools these days attach to their transcripts a school profile, describing course offerings, grading systems, and other vital statistics. Some profiles include a list of colleges the school's graduates attend.

If you are outside the area a college regularly serves, your school's profile will tell the admission office much of what it wants to know. And, for better or worse, others from your high school who preceded you to that college have compiled a record on which your school will be judged.

What does your school's record mean? If you are a very good student, nothing. If you have borderline qualifications for a college, the strength of your high school could be the deciding factor. But so could your talent on the trombone. Or your father's job. We'll look at all the borderline scale-tippers in Chapter Nine.

GRADES/CLASS RANK

After the admission officer notes what you've done, she looks at how well you've done it: your grades. She'll also want to see your class rank, which shows how well you've done compared to everyone else in your school. It will be on your transcript.

She'll look at your GPA if it's on the transcript, but only in passing. A high school GPA is virtually meaningless at a college because every school figures GPA its own way. Each has a weighting system in which grades in tougher courses such as honors and AP earn more points than grades in regular classes.

Weighting systems are similar but rarely identical. Your GPA could be 5.03—while your friend in the next town, earning the same grades in the same courses, gets a 4.26. And both are calculated on a weighted scale in which a simple "A" wins four points.

A high school GPA is virtually meaningless at a college because every school figures GPA its own way.

The admission officer wants to compare the high school records of everyone applying to her college. To do it, she quickly recalculates your GPA based on her college's formula, again giving more weight to tougher courses. But when she does it, every applicant is weighted the same.

The importance of your class rank varies by the college. Some give it considerable weight; some ignore it. Some, such as California's state universities, work on a formula in which every applicant meeting certain criteria is admitted. Class rank is one of the criteria.

Ah, you sharp readers see a contradiction. Or at least what looks like one. If class rank is important at some colleges, you ask, why shouldn't you take snap courses to grab a lot of "A's" and improve your rank?

The answer: it won't happen. Class rank usually is decided by a weighted GPA, in which tougher courses get more points. So your high school, in ranking its senior class, makes the same decisions with the same information as the college admission officer ranking her applicants.

YOUR PRIORITIES

The first information that goes on your college rating sheet reflects your high school courses and how you used them to challenge yourself. The second item reports your grades. That's the colleges' priorities and should be yours, too. Your decisions about where you spend your school days, starting in ninth grade, are among the most important you'll make.

TEST SCORES

Take the tests and take them over if you want, but not more than three times. Almost all colleges now look only at your highest score regardless of how many times you take a test.

All but a very few colleges require either the SAT or ACT as an admission prerequisite. Most now will accept either. But unless you're looking at Bowdoin, Bates, Middlebury, Union (N.Y.), or one of the few others that require no test, you'll have to take the SAT or ACT before you apply.

Despite its other uses, such as a barometer of a school's performance, the SAT is designed for one purpose: to measure a student's aptitude for college-level work. That's been its sole role for seventy years. The ACT, a little different, measures student achievement in various subject areas. Each college wants one or the other for its own purposes.

Over the years, colleges that accept both tests have devised a table to compare scores. Roughly, a 1200 SAT score equals 28 on the ACT, 1400 on the SAT is worth 32 on the ACT. Now that the SAT is changing its scoring, colleges will have to revise the comparison.

Generally, scores are used as guidelines or to set ranges. Colleges may first consider all applicants above a certain score, decide which of them should be admitted by looking at all other parts of the application, then go to the next range.

Test Prep Courses

Admission officers, when speaking candidly, say the commercial services that charge a fee to help students improve SAT/ACT scores are a waste of time and money. They don't want to provoke the wrath of the folks who run such services, so they rarely say it publicly.

Prep courses don't give you math or verbal knowledge, the essence of the SAT. They can improve your test-taking skills, teach you tricks about the technique of answering questions, and make you feel more comfortable at a test-taking desk. They can increase your test score, say, 30 points. Given the reality of the college admission process, with so many ingredients stirred into the pot, a 30-point SAT difference hardly ever is the determining factor in a decision.

The national average for repeat SAT-takers is an increase of 40 points over the first try.

Test-preparation books, on sale at most retail book outlets, offer the same help as the courses at less expense. But if you're buying a book, be careful. The SAT's content and style were changed dramatically in 1994. It now contains more open-ended questions, more attempts to measure reasoning skills. A book published before 1994 is obsolete.

You probably can do better just by taking the SAT a second time with no special preparation. The national average for repeat SAT-takers is an increase of 40 points over the first try.

SAT II Tests

Subject Tests, given in subjects such as math, science, and English, usually just after you've finished a course when the information is fresh in your mind, can help the admission officer get a feel for your true strengths. A high score in a math Subject Test, for example, could offset a lower SAT math score or a "B" in AP math.

PSAT

Taking the PSAT, a preparatory test for the SAT, is a good idea, and taking it in tenth grade could be vital to your college future as a key to merit scholarships. I explained why in Chapter Two.

ACTIVITIES

Colleges want quality, not quantity. They hope to see you interested in one or two areas, within or outside school, working hard at them, perhaps becoming a leader. A long laundry list of memberships, with no evidence of a contribution to any organization, hurts a college application more than it helps. It pegs you as a joiner or a list padder—one who wants to build up a résumé without the bother of commitment.

"We're looking for the candidates who have maxed out on the opportunities they've been provided."

When the admission officer looks at your high school activities, she'll try to translate them to her campus. She's seeking people who will add to the vitality of student life.

Were you a reporter on the school newspaper—or its editor? Were you just a member of the French club—or did you organize a French cultural event? Did you just serve on student council—or were you on a special committee created to find a way to make part of your school work better? Do you attend Junior Achievement meetings—or are you president of your company? Are you a Boy Scout—or an Eagle Scout?

She'll be looking for evidence that you're willing to use your academic talents beyond the classroom. Are you doing independent research in a biology lab? That will make your "B" in biology class

> **A long list of memberships, with no evidence of real contribution, hurts more than it helps.**

worth more than someone else's "B." If you get "A's" in Spanish, are you tutoring less adept students? Or helping with a Spanish class at an elementary school?

Do you persevere? Or do you hop from the school paper in ninth grade to the drama club in tenth to the poetry society in eleventh? If you're the latter student, your record shows a lack of focus. A long list of activities can hurt you if it's nothing more than a list. Pick activities that genuinely interest you. Stick with them and find ways to make contributions. Show the college you know how to make a difference.

If you had a part-time job that has made it difficult for you to get actively involved in many school activities, be sure to explain that on your application. Many high school students work after school or on weekends; college admission officers understand this and take it into consideration.

RECOMMENDATIONS

All colleges want letters of recommendation, at least from a teacher and a counselor. Some request, or allow you to offer, letters from friends, employers, or others who know you. Remember those key words, "who know you." Here's your chance to tell a college what it won't learn about you anywhere else. If a college doesn't ask you to write an essay, it's your only chance.

You get to pick the letter writers. Give your choices careful thought. What recommendations say, and what they don't say, often can be the key to acceptance or rejection. Over the last 15 years, I've attended decision-making meetings of admission committees at public and private colleges, from Chicago to Michigan to Penn to Boston University. I've seen committee members on the brink of a yes-or-no decision capable of going either way, looking to letters of recommendation to confirm what appear to be a student's strengths or weaknesses.

Much can be read into a letter's every word and between its lines. Students' chances can be hurt by letter writers who don't take the opportunity to be informative. Some random quotes from around the admission committee tables:

- "He recommends Todd for our consideration. There's a distinction between recommending for consideration and recommending for admission. He's making that distinction."
- "The last sentence is damning: 'Michael is definitely college material.' In a school where 99 percent of the class attends a four-year college, that should be taken for granted."
- "It's odd that someone who ought to know her so well has so little to say about her."
- "Here's a teacher who's known this individual for two years and doesn't tell us any more than we already know."
- "We're asked to take a lot on faith: 'Admit her. She's one of the best I've ever counseled.' I want to know why."

Recommendations, as you can see, are the most underrated part of your application package. They have more influence on admission decisions than most students or teachers suspect.

When you select your letter writers, try to choose a teacher and counselor who know you well within and outside the classroom. Don't be shy about telling them what you would like them to write. At the least, remind them about some of the things you've done that won't show up elsewhere in your application. And tell them why you are interested in that particular college.

An informative letter that adds to admission officers' knowledge about you can go a long way to convincing them they want you. A cliché-filled letter that says you're a good student and little more can have the opposite effect.

THE ESSAY

Every year, more and more colleges want it. So every year, more and more students spend frustrating hours worrying about what to write and how to write it. Some colleges assign a topic and ask you to write about it as part of your application. Some offer a list of topics and let you choose. Others leave it open-ended, asking you to write something about yourself.

The worst way to approach an application essay is to ignore it until it's time to write. Then the frustration can be real. You have no idea what the colleges really want you to say or what writing style they like. You get conflicting opinions from a teacher, a counselor, a friend who did it last year, and a neighbor in the newspaper business. You feel as if you're almost ready to toss the whole thing in the trash and join the Army.

The Magic Diary

Don't wait that long. For the essay, preparation can be the key to success. The best way to prepare, believe it or not, is to keep a diary. Start now, whether you're in ninth grade or eleventh, and make regular entries about what's occurring in your life each day or week.

The best way to prepare for the essay, believe it or not, is to keep a diary.

A diary, kept regularly, can have magical effects. It forces you to think about yourself, your likes and dislikes, things that are important to you and those that aren't so crucial. When the time comes to write about yourself, which is what all colleges want, you'll have an invaluable supply of notes.

Write your diary entries in whole sentences. Make sure each has a subject and verb. Resist the temptation to write in stream-of-consciousness, unconnected thoughts. It's not only good discipline, but it's good practice. When the times comes to write for the edification of admission officers, writing about yourself in a coherent style will be second nature. It won't be a frustrating, frightening new experience. You may even find, leafing back through pages of your diary, some sentences you wrote that would be an ideal first paragraph for an essay. Magic, indeed.

What They Want to Read

Whether colleges assign a topic or leave you on your own, they're looking to the essay to learn three things: how you think, how you write, and information about you they can't find anywhere else.

Think of something about which you care deeply. It could be a school project, volunteer community work, tutoring third-graders. It could be bird watching, or fishing, or tinkering in the physics lab. It could be anger that more people don't vote or pleasure that more people are recycling waste. If you feel strongly about it, you won't have to search for reasons and opinions to support your feelings. They'll be there. Then write something telling the college admission folks why you care. That's what they want to read: why you care.

Don't, whatever you do, waste their time and yours by writing an essay that summarizes all your high school accomplishments. They already have your activities list. Such an essay will add nothing and give you negative points for lack of imagination.

The essay reveals how you think and write and gives information about you they can't find elsewhere.

Admission officers won't admit it in public, but they've been known to drop an essay gingerly into the trash if it merely regurgitates information already in the application.

And don't write a travelogue. An essay on how you spent your summer vacation tells a college little about you but more about your parents' vacation tastes. It has become a cliché.

Get Her Attention

At the peak of the college application season, a typical admission officer will read almost 1,000 pages a day. If your essay causes her eyes to glaze she'll probably drop it and move on. Your challenge is to get her attention. Make her get up from her desk, walk to her colleagues, and say: "Hey, here's something you guys are going to like."

Every time an admission officer starts reading an application, he instinctively wants to admit the student. Rejection runs against human nature. But he needs some evidence that this is a student his college wants. You must provide the evidence.

MAYBE YOU'RE NOT A KID

An older student has the same 15 minutes to impress an admission officer as any other applicant. You'll submit the same application package with the same components, and perhaps a few more. But they'll be viewed a little differently.

A high school transcript and SAT/ACT scores carry less weight or may not even be required for nontraditional students, and the weight declines the longer you've been out of school. If you took the SAT in high school, a college might want your score, but it won't be looked at as closely as if you had taken the test last spring. If you didn't take it in school, you probably won't be asked to take it as an adult.

> **Your challenge is to get her attention—and get it in 15 minutes.**

Your "life experience," a favorite phrase of admission officers, makes you attractive to colleges because of the diversity it brings to the student body. Colleges think the 18-year-olds with fresh diplomas, and little life experience, can learn from associating with you. Thus the longer you've been out there and the more diverse your experiences, the less likely a weak high school record or low test score will hinder your application.

You'll probably be asked to submit a statement, perhaps as your application essay, describing what you've been doing with your life and explaining why you now wish to become a student. Read the advice above on "The Essay." It applies equally to you. If you don't have much writing experience, consider the diary tactic. Regular entries even for a few months before you apply would help make you feel comfortable writing about yourself.

Your list of community activities no doubt will be longer than a younger student's, but the same advice applies here, too.

For adult applicants, life experiences can be more important than grades and text scores.

Emphasize activities in which you have made a contribution or assumed a leadership role. Admission officers know that adults who contribute to their community are good bets to contribute to the campus.

Remember: most colleges welcome adult students with open arms for two very big reasons. One is the buyer's market. They need your tuition money because they're not getting enough from the smaller pool of high school graduates.

The second reason is expressed well by James Walters at Chapel Hill: "We see that adults are remarkably successful in college study. They come ready to do college work. They're a heckuva good bet. We give those students a decided break and I think that's true at most institutions in the country."

CHAPTER SEVEN

IT'S TIME TO APPLY

. . . painting your own best self-portrait

You sit staring at a pile of paper on your desk, wondering how long it will take to work your way through.

The pile contains applications from the 5 colleges you've selected. Each has about eight pages and that doesn't count the instructions. Your pile is fifty pages deep.

The first part of the process, finding the colleges that fit you, was fun. Now, you're thinking, comes the hard work.

Think again. It will be work, yes. And perhaps a little time-consuming because you want to do it with care. This is your one shot to formally present yourself to the colleges of your choice. You don't want to blow it. But if you're well-prepared, if you have been building an attractive record through high school, the only task now facing you is to put that record into words and numbers. Just tell them who you are and what you've done.

Despite the size of the pile, it should not be difficult.

THE COMMON APPLICATION

You might be lucky. The 5 schools you've chosen, or at least some of them, might accept the Common Application. It's an eight-page form that tells a college everything it wants to know about an applicant in a standard format.

The Common Application (reproduced starting on page 76) was devised by the National Association of Secondary School Principals (NASSP) to give the student a break. It figured a student need only paint his portrait once and send it to everyone interested, instead of poring over a different form for every college.

The idea is catching on. As the present time, more than 100 colleges accept the Common Application and the number is increasing monthly. Its popularity soared in 1994 after Harvard decided to accept it as a substitute for its own application. As is the case with so many college trends, when Harvard does it others flock to follow.

You might be lucky; all your schools might accept the Common Application.

To avoid filling out unnecessary forms, ask all the colleges on your list if the Common Application is acceptable. Its beauty, from your perspective, is that you fill it out once and then run it through a photocopier for every school on your list that takes it. (Be sure that your master is neat and clear and copy it on a good copy machine.)

If a college you're interested in accepts the Common Application, it already may have given you one. Copies also are sent each year to every high school's counseling center. If your school is out of it, check with your principal about ordering some from the NASSP's home office in Reston, Virginia. The only charge is for postage.

PAPER OR DISK?

An attractive alternative for any student who has access to a computer, also growing in popularity, is applying by means of a

> **Your counseling center probably has disks and hard copies of the Common Application.**

college-supplied computer diskette. More than half of the nation's four-year colleges offer electronic versions of their forms that can be filled out on a computer screen. Some ask just for the disk with your applications to be returned; others also want a paper printout.

You probably know by now whether or not any of your 5 colleges will take electronic applications. If they do, they have sent you either a disk or instructions on how to get one. The Common Application also is available on disk, in your counseling center or from the National Association of Secondary School Principals, 1904 Association Drive, Reston, Virginia 22091. There are companies that supply it with the application services they sell, and some college applications can be downloaded from computer networks.

A few colleges, and the number still is small, allow students to submit applications via modem directly into the school's computer. If one of your schools does so it will let you know.

But it never hurts to ask.

EARLY ADMISSION

Now comes a key decision that you already may be seriously mulling over. Two of your 5 colleges, Choosy U. and First U., offer an early admission option. The other 3 do not.

Choosy U. calls it Early Decision; First U. calls it Early Action. Basically, they're the same thing. They give you a chance to apply early, by mid-November of your senior year, and learn in December if you're accepted. Like all such programs, the details at each school are different.

In return for considering you early, Choosy insists that you agree to apply nowhere else unless it turns you down. If it accepts you in December, it wants to be sure you will enroll.

First U. has a different twist. You must agree that, if accepted on an early decision, you will immediately withdraw all other applications. It, too, wants to be sure you show up.

Both schools ask for SAT/ACT scores from eleventh grade on their early decision applications. That's no problem. You took the SAT/ACT last year. But you're wondering if an early application is wise.

First U. is your first choice. That's where you'd really like to be. You relish the prospect of applying early, being accepted, forgetting the other 4 schools, and getting on with life as a high school senior. But wait! If you apply early to First U. and get in, you must live with whatever financial aid is offered. You won't have the option of applying to Second College, Third Tech, or Nearby State to see if their financial aid packages are more generous.

While money was not an important factor when the process began, it now is a key element in your decision. You've found 4 colleges at which you can be happy and 1 you would attend if all else fails. To validly compare them, you must know how much each expects you to pay. And there's the chance, if you wait, of negotiating better financial aid deals. (More on negotiation in Chapter Nine.)

With early decision/ early action you usually apply in November and find out in December.

Your heart and mind are tugging in opposite directions. Get it over quickly or consider financial aid offers? You seek an opinion from Dad, who, being an astute parent, advises you to do whatever you think best but adds that money doesn't grow on trees. Your mind wins. You forget early decision and adjust to the idea of completing five applications.

SOME DON'TS

Let's get this out of the way; it's some advice on what not to do. You may think it's unnecessary but, based on college admission offices' experience, some college applicants need it:

- Don't use Wite-Out. A glob of white on a college application is an ugly sight to behold, especially when it's in a pile with 12 applications from neat freaks. When your crucial 15 minutes arrives, you don't want an admission officer's first thought to be of your sloppiness. If you are using a typewriter, those cute little ribbons that backspace and rub out simultaneously serve the same role as Wite-Out in a much more presentable manner.
- Don't write in longhand. You're old enough to know that most people's writing is difficult, if not impossible, to be read by anyone else. Don't make an admission officer struggle to figure out what you're saying. She may just give up and move on to the next applicant. If you don't have access to a typewriter or a computer and must use a pen, then print.
- Don't leave any question blank (unless it's labeled optional). An unanswered question denotes carelessness or something to hide, depending on the mood of the reader.
- Don't make the reader look elsewhere for an answer. For example, writing "see transcript" where the form asks for your SAT score needlessly aggravates the admission officer. She knows your SAT score will be on your transcript but she's accustomed to glancing at a certain spot on the application to find it. Not finding it there produces negative thoughts about you.
- Don't be a smart alec. "Twice a week" is not an appropriate response on the line labeled Sex. A sense of humor is desirable but there are more imaginative ways to show it.

DOING IT

Enough preliminaries. It's time to pick up the application and fill it out. Or at least half of it. You'll notice in the Common Application that only four pages are for you; four additional pages are for other people: a teacher and a counselor. You get to pick the other people.

We're going to walk through the Common Application (on page 76) because even if your colleges don't accept it, their forms will be very similar.

The first page of the application is easy. It asks for vital statistics: name, address, likely college major, etc. But there's one question that makes you pause. Just above the box requesting optional demographic data it asks if you will be a candidate for financial aid.

You think about that one. You've heard that some colleges give breaks to students who aren't applying for aid. Indeed you read somewhere about schools that say they accept full-paying students over aid-seekers.

You asked about it on your campus visits. First U. and Second College assured you their admissions are *need-blind*. That's jargon that means your financial condition isn't a factor in the admission decision. Third Tech hedged a little, saying it doesn't have enough money to cover all students' needs, but you neglected to ask what happens when the money runs out.

Now, you wonder, should you check "no" to the financial aid question (even though you are, of course, going to send in your aid application) just in case it might get you a break?

Stop wondering. You know you'll be unable to attend any of your top 3 colleges without financial help. As soon as your financial aid application arrives at First U, its financial aid computer will tell the admission office computer. If you checked "no" on your application, the admission office will know it's a lie. Offering a dishonest or willfully false answer is the same as withdrawing your application. It will be dead in the water.

On to page 2, which is more of the same: vital statistics, educational background, information about your parents. The only advice to be offered about these answers is to keep them neat. Sloppiness is not a desirable trait at admission offices.

continued on page 84

Albion • Alfred • Allegheny • American • Antioch • Babson • Bard • Barnard • Bates • Beloit • Bennington • Boston University • Bowdoin • Brandeis • Bryn Mawr • Bucknell
Carleton • Case Western Reserve • Centenary College • Centre • Claremont McKenna • Clark University • Coe • Colby • Colby-Sawyer • Colgate • Colorado College
Connecticut College • Cornell College • Denison • University of Denver • DePauw • Dickinson • Drew • Duke • Earlham • Eckerd • Elizabethtown • Elmira • Emory
Fairfield • Fisk • Fordham • Franklin & Marshall • George Washington • Gettysburg • Goucher • Grinnell • Guilford • Gustavus Adolphus • Hamilton • Hampden-Sydney
Hampshire • Hartwick • Harvard-Radcliffe   Haverford • Hobart & William Smith • Hofstra
Hollins • Hood • Johns Hopkins • Kalamazoo   Kenyon • Knox • Lafayette • Lake Forest • Lawrence
Lehigh • Lewis & Clark • Linfield • Macalester   **COMMON APPLICATION**   Manhattan • Manhattanville • University of Miami
Mills • Millsaps • Morehouse • Mount Holyoke   Muhlenberg • New York University • Oberlin
Occidental • Ohio Wesleyan • Pitzer • Pomona   University of Puget Sound • Randolph-Macon
Randolph Macon Woman's • University of Redlands   Reed College • Rensselaer Polytechnic • Rhodes
Rice • University of Richmond • Ripon • Rochester Institute of Technology • University of Rochester • Rollins • St. Lawrence • St. Olaf • Salem • Sarah Lawrence
Scripps • Simmons • Skidmore • Smith • University of the South • Southern Methodist • Southwestern • Spelman • Stetson • Susquehanna • Swarthmore
Texas Christian • Trinity College • Trinity University • Tulane • Tulsa • Union • Ursinus • Valparaiso • Vanderbilt • Vassar • Wake Forest • Washington College
Washington & Lee • Wells • Wellesley • Wesleyan • Western Maryland • Wheaton • Whitman • Whittier • Widener • Willamette • Williams • Wooster • Worcester Polytechnic

APPLICATION FOR UNDERGRADUATE ADMISSION

The colleges and universities listed above encourage the use of this application. No distinction will be made between it and the college's own form. The accompanying instructions tell you how to complete, copy, and file your application with any one or several of the colleges. Please type or print in black ink.

PERSONAL DATA

Legal name: _____
                Last   *First*   *Middle (complete)*   *Jr., etc.*   *Sex*

Prefer to be called: _____ (nickname) Former last name(s) if any: _____

Are you applying as a ☐ freshman or ☐ transfer student? For the term beginning: _____

Permanent home address: _____
                                                 Number and Street

_____
       City or Town   *County*   *State*   *Zip*

If different from the above, please give your mailing address for all admission correspondence:

Mailing address: _____
                                Number and Street

_____ Use until: _____
       City or Town   *State*   *Zip*   *Date*

Telephone at mailing address: _____ / _____ Permanent home telephone: _____ / _____
               Area Code   *Number*   *Area Code*   *Number*

Birthdate: _____ Citizenship: ☐ U.S. ☐ Permanent Resident U.S. ☐ Other _____ Visa type _____
   Month *Day* *Year*   *Country*

Possible area(s) of academic concentration/major: _____ or undecided ☐

Special college or division if applicable: _____

Possible career or professional plans: _____ or undecided ☐

Will you be a candidate for financial aid? ☐ Yes ☐ No If yes, the appropriate form(s) was/will be filed on: _____

The following items are optional: Social Security number, if any: ☐☐☐ – ☐☐ – ☐☐☐☐

Place of birth: _____ Marital status: _____
          City   *State*   *Country*

First language, if other than English: _____ Language spoken at home: _____

How would you describe yourself? Check any that apply.

☐ American Indian, Alaskan Native (tribal affiliation _____) ☐ Mexican American, Mexican

☐ Native Hawaiian, Pacific Islander ☐ African American, Black

☐ Asian American, Asian (including Indian subcontinent) (country _____) ☐ White, Anglo, Caucasian

☐ Hispanic, Latino (including Puerto Rican) (country _____) ☐ Other (Specify _____)

EDUCATIONAL DATA

School you attend now _____ Date of entry _____

Address _____ ACT/CEEB code number _____
       City   *State*   *Zip Code*

Date of secondary graduation _____ Is your school public? _____ private? _____ parochial? _____

College counselor: Name: _____ Position: _____

School telephone: _____ / _____ School FAX: _____ / _____
          Area Code   *Number*   *Area Code*   *Number*   **APP**

List all other secondary schools, including summer schools and programs you have attended beginning with ninth grade.

Name of School	Location (City, State, Zip)	Dates Attended

List all colleges at which you have taken courses for credit and list names of courses on a separate sheet. Please have a transcript sent from each institution as soon as possible.

Name of College	Location (City, State, Zip)	Degree Candidate?	Dates Attended

If not currently attending school, please check here: ☐   Describe in detail, on a separate sheet, your activities since last enrolled.

TEST INFORMATION. Be sure to note the tests required for each institution to which you are applying. The official scores from the appropriate testing agency must be submitted to each institution as soon as possible. Please list your test plans below.

	SAT I (or SAT)		SAT II: Subject Tests (or Achievement Tests)		American College Test (ACT)	Test of English as a Foreign Language (TOEFL)
Dates taken/						
to be taken						
Scores						
	Verbal	*Math*			*(Composite)*	

FAMILY

Mother's full name: _____ Is she living? _____

Home address if different from yours: _____

Occupation: _____
　　　　　(Describe briefly)　　　　　　　　　　　　　　　　*(Name of business or organization)*

Name of college (if any): _____ Degree: _____ Year: _____

Name of professional or graduate school (if any): _____ Degree: _____ Year: _____

Father's full name: _____ Is he living? _____

Home address if different from yours: _____

Occupation: _____
　　　　　(Describe briefly)　　　　　　　　　　　　　　　　*(Name of business or organization)*

Name of college (if any): _____ Degree: _____ Year: _____

Name of professional or graduate school (if any): _____ Degree: _____ Year: _____

If not with both parents, with whom do you make your permanent home: _____

Please check if parents are ☐ separated ☐ divorced ☐ other _____

Please give names and ages of your brothers or sisters. If they have attended college, give the names of the institutions attended, degrees, and approximate dates:

_____

_____

Albion • Alfred • Allegheny • American • Antioch • Babson • Bard • Barnard • Bates • Beloit • Bennington • Boston University • Bowdoin • Brandeis • Bryn Mawr • Bucknell
Carleton • Case Western Reserve • Centenary College • Centre • Claremont McKenna • Clark University • Coe • Colby • Colby-Sawyer • Colgate • Colorado College
Connecticut College • Cornell College • Denison • University of Denver • DePauw • Dickinson • Drew • Duke • Earlham • Eckerd • Elizabethtown • Elmira • Emory
Fairfield • Fisk • Fordham • Franklin & Marshall • George Washington • Gettysburg • Goucher • Grinnell • Guilford • Gustavus Adolphus • Hamilton • Hampden-Sydney
Hampshire • Hartwick • Harvard-Radcliffe   Haverford • Hobart & William Smith • Hofstra
Hollins • Hood • Johns Hopkins • Kalamazoo   Kenyon • Knox • Lafayette • Lake Forest • Lawrence
Lehigh • Lewis & Clark • Linfield • Macalester   **SCHOOL REPORT**   Manhattan • Manhattanville • University of Miami
Mills • Millsaps • Morehouse • Mount Holyoke   Muhlenberg • New York University • Oberlin
Occidental • Ohio Wesleyan • Pitzer • Pomona   University of Puget Sound • Randolph-Macon
Randolph Macon Woman's • University of Redlands   Reed College • Rensselaer Polytechnic • Rhodes
Rice • University of Richmond • Ripon • Rochester Institute of Technology • University of Rochester • Rollins • St. Lawrence • St. Olaf • Salem • Sarah Lawrence
Scripps • Simmons • Skidmore • Smith • University of the South • Southern Methodist • Southwestern • Spelman • Stetson • Susquehanna • Swarthmore
Texas Christian • Trinity College • Trinity University • Tulane • Tulsa • Union • Ursinus • Valparaiso • Vanderbilt • Vassar • Wake Forest • Washington College
Washington & Lee • Wells • Wellesley • Wesleyan • Western Maryland • Wheaton • Whitman • Whittier • Widener • Willamette • Williams • Wooster • Worcester Polytechnic

SECONDARY SCHOOL COUNSELOR EVALUATION

The colleges and universities listed above encourage the use of this form. No distinction will be made between it and the college's own form. The accompanying instructions tell you how to complete, copy, and file your application with any one or several of the colleges. Please type or print in black ink.

TO THE APPLICANT:

After filling in the information below, give this form to your college counselor.

Student name: _____
          Last   *First*   *Middle (complete)*   *Jr. etc.*

Address: _____
          Street   *City*   *State*   *Zip*

Social Security No. (optional) _____

Current Year Courses—Please indicate title, level, and term of all courses you are taking this year: _____

_____

_____

_____

Please detach along perforation

TO THE SECONDARY SCHOOL COLLEGE COUNSELOR:

After filling in the blanks below, use both sides of this form to describe the applicant.

This candidate ranks _____ in a class of _____ students and has a cumulative grade point average of _____ on a _____ scale.

The rank covers a period from _____ to _____. If a precise rank is not available, please indicate rank to the
                                (mo./yr.)   *(mo./yr.)*

nearest tenth from the top. The rank is weighted _____ unweighted _____. How many students share this rank _____

Of this candidate's graduating class, _____% plan to attend a four-year college.

In comparison to other college preparatory students *at our school,* the applicant's course selection is:
          ☐ most demanding   ☐ demanding   ☐ average   ☐ less than demanding.

How long have you known the applicant, and in what context? _____

What are the first words that come to your mind to describe the applicant? _____

_____

Counselor's name (please print or type): _____ _____
                                                                                    Signature

Position: _____ School: _____

School address: _____ Date: _____

Office telelephone: _____/_____ Office FAX: _____/_____
                Area Code   *Number*   *Area Code*   *Number*

School CEEB/ACT Code ☐ ☐ ☐ ☐ ☐ ☐

Please Note: Attach applicant's official transcript, including courses in progress. Include, if available, a school profile and transcript legend.
(Please check transcript copies for readability.)
                                                                                    (See reverse side) **SR**

Please feel free to write whatever you think is important about this student, including a description of academic and personal characteristics. We are particularly interested in the candidate's intellectual promise, motivation, relative maturity, integrity, independence, originality, initiative, leadership potential, capacity for growth, special talents, and enthusiasm. We welcome information that will help us to differentiate this student from others.

(Optional) I recommend this student: ☐ With reservation ☐ Fairly strongly ☐ Strongly ☐ Enthusiastically

CONFIDENTIALITY:

We value your comments highly and ask that you complete this form in the knowledge that it may be retained in the student's file should the applicant matriculate at a member college. In accordance with the Family Educational Rights and Privacy Act of 1974, matriculating students do have access to their permanent files which may include forms such as this one. Colleges do not provide access to admissions records to applicants, those students who are denied admission, or those students who decline an offer of admission. Again, your comments are important to us and we thank you for your cooperation. These colleges are committed to administer all educational policies and activities without discrimination on the basis of race, color, religion, national or ethnic origin, age, handicap, or sex. The admissions process at private undergraduate institutions is exempt from the federal regulation implementing Title IX of the Education Amendments of 1972.

Albion • Alfred • Allegheny • American • Antioch • Babson • Bard • Barnard • Bates • Beloit • Bennington • Boston University • Bowdoin • Brandeis • Bryn Mawr • Bucknell
Carleton • Case Western Reserve • Centenary College • Centre • Claremont McKenna • Clark University • Coe • Colby • Colby-Sawyer • Colgate • Colorado College
Connecticut College • Cornell College • Denison • University of Denver • DePauw • Dickinson • Drew • Duke • Earlham • Eckerd • Elizabethtown • Elmira • Emory
Fairfield • Fisk • Fordham • Franklin & Marshall • George Washington • Gettysburg • Goucher • Grinnell • Guilford • Gustavus Adolphus • Hamilton • Hampden-Sydney
Hampshire • Hartwick • Harvard-Radcliffe
Hollins • Hood • Johns Hopkins • Kalamazoo
Lehigh • Lewis & Clark • Linfield • Macalester
Mills • Millsaps • Morehouse • Mount Holyoke
Occidental • Ohio Wesleyan • Pitzer • Pomona
Randolph Macon Woman's • University of Redlands

TEACHER EVALUATION

Haverford • Hobart & William Smith • Hofstra
Kenyon • Knox • Lafayette • Lake Forest • Lawrence
Manhattan • Manhattanville • University of Miami
Muhlenberg • New York University • Oberlin
University of Puget Sound • Randolph-Macon
Reed College • Rensselaer Polytechnic • Rhodes

Rice • University of Richmond • Ripon • Rochester Institute of Technology • University of Rochester • Rollins • St. Lawrence • St. Olaf • Salem • Sarah Lawrence
Scripps • Simmons • Skidmore • Smith • University of the South • Southern Methodist • Southwestern • Spelman • Stetson • Susquehanna • Swarthmore
Texas Christian • Trinity College • Trinity University • Tulane • Tulsa • Union • Ursinus • Valparaiso • Vanderbilt • Vassar • Wake Forest • Washington College
Washington & Lee • Wells • Wellesley • Wesleyan • Western Maryland • Wheaton • Whitman • Whittier • Widener • Willamette • Williams • Wooster • Worcester Polytechnic

The colleges and universities listed above encourage the use of this form. No distinction will be made between it and the college's own form. The accompanying instructions tell you how to complete, copy, and file your application with any one or several of the colleges. Please type or print in black ink.

STUDENT:
Fill in the information below and give this form and a stamped envelope, addressed to each college to which you are applying that requests a Teacher Evaluation, to a teacher who has taught you an academic subject.

Student name: _____
          Last   *First*   *Middle (complete)*

Address: _____

TEACHER:
The Common Application group of colleges finds candid evaluations helpful in choosing from among highly qualified candidates. We are primarily interested in whatever you think is important about the applicant's academic and personal qualifications for college. Please submit your references promptly. A photocopy of this reference form, or another reference you may have prepared on behalf of this student is acceptable. You are encouraged to keep the original of this form in your private files for use should the student need additional recommendations. We are grateful for your assistance.

CONFIDENTIALITY:
We value your comments highly and ask that you complete this form in the knowledge that it may be retained in the student's file should the applicant matriculate at a member college. In accordance with the Family Educational Rights and Privacy Act of 1974, matriculating students do have access to their permanent files which may include forms such as this one. Colleges do not provide access to admissions records to applicants, those students who are denied admission, or those students who decline an offer of admission. Again, your comments are important to us and we thank you for your cooperation. These colleges are committed to administer all educational policies and activities without discrimination on the basis of race, color, religion, national or ethnic origin, age, handicap, or sex. The admissions process at private undergraduate institutions is exempt from the federal regulation implementing Title IX of the Education Amendments of 1972.

Please detach along perforation

Please return a photocopy of this sheet to the appropriate admissions office(s) in the envelope(s) provided you by this student.

Teacher's Name (please print or type) _____ Position _____

Secondary School _____

School Address _____
        Street   *City*   *State*   *Zip*

BACKGROUND INFORMATION

How long have you known this student and in what context? _____

What are the first words that come to your mind to describe this student? _____

_____

List the courses you have taught this student, noting for each the student's year in school (10th, 11th, 12th) and the level of course difficulty (AP, accelerated, honors, elective, etc.). _____

_____

(See reverse side) **TE**

EVALUATION

Please feel free to write whatever you think is important about this student, including a description of academic and personal characteristics. We are particularly interested in the candidate's intellectual promise, motivation, relative maturity, integrity, independence, originality, initiative, leadership potential, capacity for growth, special talents, and enthusiasm. We welcome information that will help us to differentiate this student from others.

RATINGS

Compared to other college-bound students whom you have taught, check how you would rate this student in terms of academic skills and potential:

No basis		Below Average	Average	Good (above average)	Very Good (well above average)	Excellent (top 10%)	One of the top few encountered in my career
	Creative, original thought						
	Motivation						
	Independence, initiative						
	Intellectual ability						
	Academic achievement						
	Written expression of ideas						
	Effective class discussion						
	Disciplined work habits						
	Potential for growth						
	SUMMARY EVALUATION						

Signature _____ Date _____

ACADEMIC HONORS

Briefly describe any scholastic distinctions or honors you have won beginning with ninth grade:

_____

_____

_____

EXTRACURRICULAR, PERSONAL, AND VOLUNTEER ACTIVITIES

Please list your principal extracurricular, community, and family activities and hobbies in the order of their interest to you. Include specific events and/or major accomplishments such as musical instrument played, varsity letters earned, etc. Please (✓) in the right column those activities you hope to pursue in college.

Activity	Grade level or post-secondary (p.s.) 9 10 11 12 PS	Approximate time spent Hours per week / Weeks per year	Positions held, honors won, or letters earned	Do you plan to participate in college?

WORK EXPERIENCE

List any job (including summer employment) you have held during the past three years.

Specific nature of work	Employer	Approximate dates of employment	Approximate no. of hours spent per week

In the space provided below, briefly discuss which of these activities (extracurricular and personal activities or work experience) has had the most meaning for you, and why.

_____

_____

_____

_____

_____

PERSONAL STATEMENT

This personal statement helps us become acquainted with you in ways different from courses, grades, test scores, and other objective data. *It enables you to demonstrate your ability to organize thoughts and express yourself. Please write an essay about one of the topics listed below.* You may attach extra pages (same size, please) if your essay exceeds the limits of this page.

1) Evaluate a significant experience or achievement that has special meaning to you.
2) Discuss some issue of personal, local, or national concern and its importance to you.
3) Indicate a person who has had a significant influence on you, and describe that influence.

I understand that: (1) it is my responsibility to report any changes in my schedule to the colleges to which I am applying, and (2) *if I am an Early Action or Early Decision Candidate, that I must attach a letter with this application notifying that college of my intent.*

My signature below indicates that all information in my application is complete, factually correct, and honestly presented.

Signature _____ Date _____

These colleges are committed to administer all educational policies and activities without discrimination on the basis of race, color, religion, national or ethnic origin, age, handicap, or sex. The admissions process at private undergraduate institutions is exempt from the federal regulation implementing Title IX of the Education Amendments of 1972.

AWARDS

Remove pages 3–6 and set them aside to be delivered to the people you've selected at your schools. Next for you in the application is page 7. This looks like another simple recitation of personal facts but it's a little more. It's one place where an admission officer learns about your ability, or willingness, to follow instructions.

At the top of the page, it asks for your academic honors beginning in ninth grade. Don't lead the list with the National Honor Society even if you consider it your most significant recognition. Start with the earliest high school awards and move on to the most recent. Some admission officers won't pay attention to the order of your list. Others will. Don't take a chance. Do it the way it's requested.

Don't be afraid to continue your answer to any question on a separate sheet of paper. The admission officer wants to see your whole record in a readable form. Don't try to crunch it into the allotted space if it won't fit.

List your awards in the order you received them, not in the order you think of them.

And don't list as awards those psuedo-recognition programs conducted by publishers who will print your name in a directory if you buy a copy. Every admission officer knows those programs for what they are: publishers' marketing tools. As one admission officer puts it: "Don't be tricked into giving them your money for something that will be meaningless to your future."

ACTIVITIES

Next comes your list of activities within and outside school. This will get much more scrutiny than your awards list.

Admission officers look quickly at that column on the right labeled "Positions held, honors won, or letters earned." They want to see not a list of activities but a list of significant contributions, evidence of a commitment, to even one or two endeavors. (Note: "Positions held" does not mean halfback or third base.)

Again, pay attention. The college wants you to tell how strongly you feel about each activity by the order in which you list it. The instructions clearly ask you to rank your activities "in the order of their interest to you." This is a ranking that most admission officers look at very carefully. If it's obvious that you didn't follow instructions, it counts against you.

I remember well an admission committee member holding up an application with a look of disdain and commenting: "He says the newspaper is his most significant activity and he left it after ninth grade." The application went nowhere.

List everything significant that you've done in school, at your church, organizations such as Girl Scouts and Junior Achievement, and community volunteer work. Be sure those for which you have something to report under "Positions, honors, etc." are listed high. Remember, laundry lists are useless.

They want to see a list of *significant* contributions to even just one or two endeavors.

If you are leaning at all toward continuing an activity in college, check the box that says you plan to participate. Admission officers seek students who will contribute to their campuses beyond the classroom. A desire to take part in college activities always is considered favorably.

JOBS

The Work Experience section asks for any jobs you've held after school or in the summer for the last three years, or since you entered ninth grade. This, too, is looked at closely. Your employment can be a mitigating factor if you show few strong commitments to extra-curricular activities.

Your jobs also can help convince an admission officer that you're sincerely interested in an activity. If you've spent four years in the school drama club and work in the summer at a community theater, that's evidence of a strong interest in theater.

YOUR TURN

At last you get a chance to say something instead of just answering questions. At the bottom of the page you have an opportunity to explain in your own words which of all the awards, activities, and jobs listed above has the most meaning for you.

Pick one item from all on the page that has indeed meant the most and say why. Let your feelings come through. It could be the National Honor Society, which you feel is a culmination of all that you tried to do in high school. It could be the school newspaper, which you transformed into a publication students respect. It could be your work at a homeless shelter in which you feel you're giving something back to the community. *Something* you have done in the last three years means a lot to you. Write about it.

An Ivy League school once accepted an applicant who had been borderline because she used this statement to describe a sincere interest in playing the flute and explained what the flute meant to her.

The statement doesn't have to be a major essay. It can be just a few sentences to fill the space on the application form or two paragraphs on a separate sheet of paper. But write it with care. The admission officer certainly will read it with care for several reasons. She wants to know what you feel strongly about and what type of experience evokes strong emotions. She also will read it, as she will your formal essay, to see how you express yourself in writing.

In many admission offices, especially at more selective colleges, this little piece of writing is considered a second essay. It is compared, often side by side, with your main essay to give the reader a feel for what interests you, how you think, and how you write.

If you are a good writer capable of turning a beautiful phrase, but only if you work hard at it and give it long thought, give this little statement some long thought. And if you show your best writing in your essay then slough off the meaningful activity statement with a couple of mundane sentences, the contrast quickly will be apparent. Questions will flow through the admission officer's mind. One of them might well be: who wrote the essay for you?

THE ESSAY

You've been thinking about it for months, working on it for weeks. Now it's the moment of truth when you must put the finished version neatly on page 8 or attach it as a separate sheet. The application calls it a Personal Statement. Students everywhere know it as The Essay.

"Write about something you care about."

We looked at some ways to prepare for the essay, select a topic, and become comfortable writing about yourself earlier. (Remember the magic diary?) Some of that advice, especially about the topic, deserves rereading; refer back to Chapter Six.

The application means what it says. Pay attention to the requested length; if it says 500 words, don't write 1,000. The college wants to know more about you than it has learned so far. Among the things it wants to know, and it says so in italics so you won't miss it, is how you think and how you write. This is your chance to show the college how you think, how you write, and something about your feelings, your desires, your goals, or your interests that doesn't show up on page 7.

The introduction on page 8 offers three broad categories into which your essay can fall. Think about each of them. Somewhere in one of those three areas is a topic you can use to tell something about yourself.

The guidelines suggest you can evaluate an experience or achievement that has meaning for you. The key words there are "evaluate" and "meaning." A narrative about a summer trip to Europe or a month's camp-out in the Everglades won't reveal anything about you unless you explain why it was important or what you personally achieved from it.

"We look for insights, for glimpses of one's individual characteristics," says Gary Ripple of Lafayette College. "Grammar and basic writing style are essential." If grammar is not your strong point, have an English teacher, a parent, or a friend who knows grammatical rules check your final version.

An admission officer at the University of Chicago once voted against an applicant because her essay "jumps from activity to activity to activity and as soon as I'm interested she switches to something else."

"Grammar and basic writing style are essential."

Worth David, longtime dean of admissions at Yale and now retired, offered this advice: "Write about something you care about. We don't particularly care what that is. It might be about the failure of people to vote in local elections or why fly-fishing is exciting. But show us that you care."

And an admission officer at the University of Pennsylvania who reads dozens of essays a day in her busy season has this advice: "There are real people on the other side of the desk reading your application. Talk to us."

BACK TO SCHOOL

The hard part is over. You've done your absolute best with the essay and "meaningful activity" statement. All questions on your part of the application are answered. If you haven't done so yet, you now must take the other half of the application to school.

Of the four pages you set aside, two go to a counselor and two to a teacher. That's standard practice. Most colleges want to hear about you from both perspectives. If a college that accepts the Common Application desires more than those two recommendations, it will let you know.

You likely won't have much choice of a counselor to submit a recommendation. You'll probably be expected to use the one as-signed to work with you. But if you have a choice, pick the one who knows you best as a person as well as a student.

Even if you don't have a choice of counselor, you certainly can select a teacher to recommend you. You probably already have one in mind. It's a teacher you respect, with whom you've established a solid rapport and worked with in an after-school activity, who knows you are more than someone sitting at a classroom desk. It's a teacher with whom you have a comfortable relationship, who you feel certain would present an accurate—maybe even flattering—picture of you to the colleges.

It won't hurt to remind your teachers and counselors of some of your high school accomplishments.

Take the two-page recommendation form to the teacher when he has a few minutes to chat. Tell him about the colleges to which you're apply-ing. Give him a copy of the four pages you've prepared. Explain why you've selected your essay topic, what you are trying to tell the college about yourself. Ask if he'll help you deliver the message. And don't ask her two days before the deadline. Give her at least one month's notice.

It won't hurt to remind the teacher, and the counselor who will be writing your recommendation, of some of your high school accom-plishments just in case they didn't know or have forgotten. You might even want to make a list of things you've done to jog their memories. Teachers and counselors say they appreciate such remind-ers when they're asked to write recommendations. They can't share information about you with the college if they don't have it.

It's highly possible that those say-nothing recommendations getting the bad reviews in Chapter Six came from counselors and teachers who knew very little about the students. If your teacher knows you, and is sincerely interested in helping you, he'll know what to say to help. But just in case, remind him as I've reminded you and as admission officers remind all of us. In the recommendations, as with the essay, they would like to learn something about you that they don't already know.

Your applications are complete and in the mail. Your counselor will send your high school transcript to each of your five colleges.

NOW WHAT HAPPENS?

Three of your 5 colleges—First U., Second College, and Choosy U.—are what the admission officers call May 1 schools. They're among the large group, including the nation's most selective, that agree to use a May 1 deadline for students to accept offers of admission. They make their decisions after all applicants have been considered, scored, and perhaps debated around an admission committee table.

Although they'll never know it, some students may be accepted and rejected two or three times as the admission staff tries to balance its freshman class by all sorts of desirable measures: gender, ethnicity, geography, socioeconomic status, even in some cases a student's likely major.

The May 1 schools don't, however, notify applicants at the same time (although all 8 of the Ivy League schools do agree on a common notification date). Your 3 colleges try to get letters in the mail between mid-March and April 1. Third Tech and Nearby State use a rolling admissions policy. Applications are accepted or rejected as they arrive until the freshman class is full.

On February 18, you receive the first letter. You have been accepted at Nearby State. You're neither surprised nor excited. Your "safety valve" school is safe indeed.

A week later, a letter comes from Third Tech. You open it with a mixture of confidence and fear. You thought they liked you there, but . . . and then a large sigh of relief. Third Tech is inviting you to be one of next year's freshmen. You've made it to one of your top 3. That makes the monthlong wait to hear from the May 1 schools a little easier.

It's a month to the day when you come home from school to see the First U. envelope in the mail. Your heart starts pumping a little faster. The letter is thick, which usually means good news because it contains acceptance papers. (Rejections are one-page letters.) You sit down to open this one. Yes, the news is good: "I am delighted to inform you that we are offering you admission to. . . ." It's over. Your top-choice college wants you. All the work was worth the result. Now you can coast through the summer.

In rolling admissions, applications are accepted or rejected as they arrive until the class is full.

Whoa! Back up a minute. There's still that little matter of paying for it. First U.'s tuition is $16,000 and there's room and board, books, and other stuff on top of that. Dad can't write a check for that much money. And you've not yet heard from First U. about financial aid. (As a matter of fact, you haven't heard about financial aid from any of the schools yet.)

You read the letter carefully. Near the bottom is the news that you will receive a financial aid award letter in about 10 days. Your future is still uncertain. You must wait a while longer.

Meanwhile, Second College checks in. It also has accepted you. Four out of 4.

Then comes Choosy U. It regrets to inform you that it can't offer you a spot right now but has placed you on its Wait List. If enough admitted students don't accept by May 1, Choosy will go to its Wait List for replacements. If you'd like to stay on the Wait List, it asks you to sign and return the enclosed form. Choosy was your "reach" school. You didn't think you'd make it but you wanted to try. You feel good that you weren't rejected outright but placed in the "maybe later" category.

But you have 4 schools now to choose from.

THE WAIT LIST

Your chances of clearing the Wait List and getting an offer vary widely with the school and the year. Some colleges use a Wait List to test the interest of borderline applicants. They intend to take, say, the first 25 or 30 who ask to remain on the list. Others rarely move anyone off the Wait List and use it simply as a consolation prize for students who just missed.

If another school, say First U., had placed you on its Wait List your decision would be tougher. Do you accept a firm offer from Second College or Third Tech that requires a payment on tuition and a fee to hold a dorm room? Or wait to see what First U. does? Or both?

The first thing to do is send in First U.'s form saying you want to stay on the list. If it's using the Wait List to test the sincerity of your interest, an acceptance could be in the return mail.

Then talk to your counselor. She may have had experience with other students on First U.'s Wait List and can assess your chances of eventually clearing it. Or she may know someone at First U. who can make the same assessment.

Call the First U. admission office (but be patient, the phones probably will be busy). Ask the admission officer with whom you had the nice chat during your visit if she can tell you when a decision might be made. Explain that First U. is your first choice but you might have to go with your second or third choice instead of waiting several weeks to find out if you've moved from Wait List to acceptance. If you are candid with her, she likely will respond in the same manner.

If you get no reasonably firm assurance that you eventually will be accepted, you're better off forgetting First U. The fact of life is that most applicants on Wait Lists never get off.

NOW YOU WAIT FOR THE MONEY

But for you, this is a hypothetical problem. You have been accepted by 4 colleges, including your first choice. You have no desire to wait for Choosy U. You tear up its Wait List acceptance form and drop it in the trash.

Your decision about where you'll go to college now depends on money. It still won't be the only factor but you can't decide until you know how much each expects you to pay.

Each of the 4 will expect you to pay a different amount. We'll see how they came up with those numbers in Chapter Eight.

As you wait, meanwhile, you think about your visits to each of those campuses, what you liked about them and didn't like. You wonder if it might be wise to drop in again to refresh your memory.

You again read First U.'s letter. It invites you to a campus reception for admitted applicants before you must make a decision to enroll. You accept the invitation. And you decide that if the financial aid offers are about equal, you might revisit Second College and Third Tech, too.

MAYBE YOU AREN'T A KID

The application process for adults varies with the college. Some have separate forms for older students. Others use the same form but want to know that you are "nontraditional."

When you visit the admission office you'll learn what it wants. It may forgo niceties such as an SAT score in exchange for additional essays describing your life experiences in the adult world. Those experiences can add much-desired diversity to a college's overall student body.

CHAPTER EIGHT

FINDING THE MONEY

. . . 2 of 3 students don't pay the sticker price

The price tag scares you. Despite all the reassurances in his book and elsewhere that you probably can afford the college of your choice, you're still worried. You saw that table in Chapter One listing the colleges that charge more than $25,000 just for tuition, room, and board, and you know your parents can't come up with that kind of money.

Don't panic. There's help out there. The help is called financial aid. That may scare you, too. You have heard stories from friends in college, or from their parents, about how difficult and traumatic the financial aid process is. Yes, it takes some work. But, hey, money isn't free. And it's less work than completing those five college applications you just put in the mail. And, yes, there's some trauma in telling strangers how much money you have and where you keep it. But it's the same information you give every year to those strangers at the IRS, and they don't help pay your college bills.

There is enough to be said about the financial aid process to fill a whole book. (And I've written one; it looks very much like this one on your bookstore shelf.) Just in case your bookstore is closed

THE SHIFTING AID POT

Here's a comparison of trends in the three major sources of financial aid—
the federal government, states, and colleges—over the last 10 years.

	Dollars Awarded (in millions)		
	1984	1989	1994
All federal programs	13,413	18,455	19,181
Pell Grants	3,033	4,471	5,683
Work-Study	645	625	760
Perkins Loans	677	874	903
State grant programs	1,222	1,581	2,429
Institutional aid	2,556	3,978	8,081
All financial aid	18,948	25,511	41,935

Source: The College Board

when you're reading this, or someone else has the only car, I'll tell you everything I said in *USA TODAY Financial Aid for College* but in less detail. (Well, maybe not *everything*.)

THE RUMORS

You've undoubtedly heard the rumors along with the financial aid horror stories. They seem to be increasingly prevalent in all parts of the country. They come in three categories: 1) financial aid is complicated; 2) it's only available to the poor; and 3) aid recipients are second-class citizens. All three rumors are false.

Rumor One

Applying for financial aid is one of the easiest tasks confronting you in the entire college-finding process. It's a lot easier than making those lists from directories, setting up campus visits, or writing an essay.

You'll fill a four-page form with numbers that you and your parents also will use on your tax returns. And you'll do it only once. The federal government produces a form that in effect is a Common Application for financial aid accepted by every college. The gov-

WHY SOME GET A BREAK

Almost one third (32 percent) of colleges responding to a 1994 survey report they make financial aid packages more attractive for certain students. Their reasons show a clash in priorities between public and private colleges. Here are the top five reasons, by public and private schools, for offering a better financial aid package.

Public Colleges
Offer better aid packages to attract students of:

Desirable ethnicity	75%
Academic merit	72%
Low income	39%
Athletic ability	33%
Music, art, theater talent	16%

Private Colleges
Offer better aid packages to attract students of:

Academic merit	91%
Desirable ethnicity	52%
Music, art, theater talent	39%
Athletic ability	30%
Low income	29%

Source: National Association of College Admission Counselors

ernment sends the information on your application to every school on your list. Yes, some schools will want more information and send you supplemental forms. They're easy to handle, too.

Determining your eligibility for financial aid also is relatively easy. You find two numbers and subtract one from the other. One number is the cost of attending a college. That you already know. The other number, which can be calculated by anyone who knows how to figure percentages, is the amount you and your family are expected to pay.

The subtraction produces a magic number, your financial Need. That's Need with a capital "N" because it's a number that's used throughout the financial aid process to help people decide what financial help you will and will not receive.

Rumor Two

Some government programs provide financial aid only to the most needy students. But the $42 billion given away by government and colleges last year went to students at all levels of the economic spectrum.

If you visit Gettysburg (Pa.) College, you can pick up a brochure that tells you 66 percent of the freshmen receiving aid last year had family incomes over $50,000, and 13 percent were from families with six-figure incomes. That's not an unusual percentage for a private college in Gettysburg's $24,000-plus price range.

The eligibility formula, that simple subtraction of one number from another, is devised so even wealthy families can wind up with a financial Need.

Rumor Three

If aid recipients are second-class citizens, every campus would have a large second class. Remember those numbers from Chapter One. At 746 colleges reporting such information, 63 percent of the freshmen are receiving aid. Two of every 3 freshmen get it.

Applying for aid is often the easiest part of the whole college selection and admission process.

YOUR MAGIC NUMBER

Your key to the financial aid vaults is that magic number, your financial Need. It usually bears little resemblance to the amount of money you need to attend a college but it's a number you must have to start the process.

The higher your number the better, because it represents, in dollars, the maximum amount of aid for which you're eligible. If a college really wants you, however, maximums are flexible.

MAGIC NUMBER WORKSHEET
TO ESTIMATE YOUR EXPECTED FAMILY CONTRIBUTION

(Income and taxes are for year before the application is filed. For example, applicants in winter/spring 1996 use 1995 figures.)

Parents' Contribution

  I. Income

      Parents' adjusted gross income $ _____

      Untaxed income, including IRA contribution   + _____

        Total Income   _____ (A)

  II. Allowances

      Federal income tax   + _____

      State, other taxes   + _____

      Social Security taxes   + _____

      Employment allowance (see text)   + _____

      Income protected (see text)   + _____

        Total Allowances   _____ (B)

  III. Available Income (Line A - Line B)   _____ (C)

  IV. Assets

      Cash in bank accounts _____

      Investment equity (excluding residence)   + _____

      Business net worth   + _____

      Net Worth   _____

      Asset protection allowance (see text)   − _____

      Discretionary Net Worth (DNW)   _____

  V. Available Assets (12% of DNW)   _____ (D)

  VI. Adjusted Available Income (Line C + Line D)   _____ (E)

  VII. Parents' Total Contribution (see next table)   _____

Parents' Contribution to Student   _____ (F)
  (Parents' contribution divided by number of
  family members in college)

Student's Contribution

  I. Income

      Student's adjusted gross income   _____

      Untaxed income   + _____

        Total Income   _____ (G)

  II. Allowances

      Federal income tax   _____

      State, other taxes   + _____

      Social Security taxes   + _____

      Income protected   + $1,750

        Total Allowances   _____ (H)

  III. Available Income (Line G - Line H)   _____ (I)

  IV. Contribution from income (50% of Line I)   _____ (J)

  V. Assets (cash in banks, investment equity)   _____ (K)

  VI. Contribution from assets (35% of Line K)   _____ (L)

Student's Contribution (Line J + Line L)   _____ (M)

Expected Family Contribution (Line F + Line M)   _____

CALCULATING PARENTS'
TOTAL CONTRIBUTION

If Line E (above) is*	Parents' contribution is
–$3,408 or less	–$750
–$3,409 to $9,700	22% of Line E
$9,701 to $12,200	$2,134 + 25% of Line E over $9,700
$12,201 to $14,600	$2,759 + 29% of Line E over $12,200
$14,601 to $17,100	$3,455 + 34% of Line E over $14 600
$17,101 to $19,600	$4,305 + 40% of Line E over $17,100
$19,601 or more	$5,305 + 47% of Line E over $19,600

* Can be a negative number

Your Need is the result of the simple subtraction mentioned earlier. You find the cost of the college to which you're applying and subtract the amount your family is expected to pay.

The variable is the college cost. Your family's expected contribution remains the same wherever you go. Because no 2 colleges' costs are identical, your Need will differ with each application. The **Even wealthy families can wind up with a financial Need.** more expensive the school, the higher your magic number.

If the subtraction produces a negative number—if your expected family contribution is greater than the college cost—you officially have no Need. That doesn't mean you won't get aid. Some aid is available for everyone, even no-Need folks.

Most students don't worry in advance about their Need. They send in their financial aid application and wait for a computer to mail them a notice announcing their Expected Family Contribution (EFC). Then they moan in anguish about how this stupid computer expects them to spend their entire savings for one year of college.

As they moan, they overlook two facts that perhaps they never knew: 1) your financial Need determined by a formula often is not even close to the money you really need; 2) your Expected Family Contribution often is not even close to the money you'll have to pay.

Both numbers are starting points. The eventual real numbers depend on many things, including how much a college wants you.

FINDING THE COST

If you're a student or parent who likes to plan in advance and would rather not wait for the computer mailing, here's a look at how to figure your magic number on your pocket calculator.

The college cost used in your magic number subtraction is what the aid people call Cost of Attendance. That's more than just tuition, room, and board. It's every dollar you'll spend to go to First U., Second College, or Third Tech—including books, transportation, laundry, and toothpaste.

Most major directories now include an estimated Cost of Attendance for every college. It typically will be broken down into tuition,

The more expensive the college, the higher your Need will be.

fees, room and board, books and supplies, transportation, and "other." (Other is laundry and toothpaste.) Add those numbers and you'll be pretty close to your cost of attendance.

At Yale, tuition, room, and board are $26,350, but its cost of attendance listed in a major directory is more than $2,000 higher: $28,460. That difference is typical. After you pay tuition, room, and board (or just tuition if you're staying at home), expect to spend $1,000 to $2,500 more for all the incidentals. When the financial aid formula figures your Need, the incidentals count.

Dependent or Independent?

To find your Expected Family Contribution, you first must know how the computer looks at your financial condition when it applies the formula. You'll either be dependent and your parents' income and assets must be considered, or independent and only your money counts. In most cases, an independent student has more Need. But in most cases, the student is a dependent.

In the past, the line was fuzzy, but in 1992, Congress drew it more clearly. Now to be considered independent you must answer "yes" to one of six questions:

- Are you 24 or older?
- Are you married?
- Are you a graduate or professional student?
- Do you have dependents?
- Are you an orphan or ward of a court?
- Are you a military veteran?

One "yes" and you're independent. Answer "no" six times and you're dependent.

The rules have obvious inconsistencies. If you join the Army at 18, serve two years, come home and again are totally dependent on your parents, you're still independent for financial aid purposes as a military veteran. It's the 1990s version of the G.I. bill.

Finding your contribution

Your Expected Family Contribution (EFC) is the sum of what you and your parents are expected to pay for a year at college based on income and assets. If you're independent, only your income and assets go into the calculation.

For this example, I'll assume you're dependent. (I'll talk about independents at the end of the chapter under Maybe You're Not a Kid.) I'll also assume you live in Nicetown, Pennsylvania, and both your parents are 45. The numbers will vary slightly with your state and your parents' age.

Look at the worksheet on page 98. It's not as complicated as it first seems.

Section I asks for your parents' income, the same numbers they'll report to the IRS. Section II lets you deduct some stuff. Enter the total income taxes your parents paid. For state taxes take 6 percent of their income, the amount allowed to Pennsylvanians. If both parents work, take an Employment Allowance of $2,500 or 35 percent of the lower earner's annual salary, whichever is less. If only one works, use that salary. Add up the allowances, subtract them from income and you have their income available to pay for college.

In Section IV, list your parents' assets. Then take an asset protection allowance of $36,300 because your older parent is 45. (The allowance ranges from zero if your parent is younger than 26 to $66,300 for a parent 65 or older.) Subtract the allowance from your parents' net worth and you'll have the amount of their assets considered available to pay for college.

Go through the simple calculations in Lines V and VI. Then check the table Calculating Parents' Total Contribution to see how much of their income should go to their kids' tuition. Divide it by the number of family members in college. That's your parents' expected contribution to your education next year.

Follow the similar self-explanatory steps to find your contribution as a student. Add it to your parents' contribution and, presto, there's your EFC. Easy, wasn't it?

It won't be a precise number unless you live in Pennsylvania and your older parent is 45. But it will be in the ballpark, giving you an advance-planning idea of your eventual financial Need. (If you'd like a precise number, tables listing all the deductions and allowances should be available at a well-equipped high school counseling center and any college financial aid office. They're also in my other book, *USA TODAY Financial Aid for College*.)

Now subtract your EFC from the cost of the 5 colleges you have selected and you have your five magic numbers: your Need that will help decide how much aid you get if you're accepted.

THE PROFILE

It might be possible, if you're applying to the right school at the right time, to have someone else's computer do those advance-planning calculations.

A new player in the game is scheduled to appear at some schools in the fall of 1995 and likely will show up elsewhere later. It's called the Financial Aid PROFILE. (Otherwise known as the PROFILE.) It's a service of The College Board that will allow you to submit financial data early in your senior year, get an estimate of your Need, and also complete a customized financial aid application. It will be available if you're applying to be admitted in September 1996 or later to a college that subscribes to the new service.

In addition to helping students, the PROFILE will provide supplemental information to colleges and some private scholarship programs that want more than they get on the government's form. When it's working as planned, students can use the PROFILE to apply for aid to any subscribing college. But it's merely a supplement to, not a replacement for, the basic government application. Students who qualify for federal aid will also have to complete the FAFSA.

THE MANY KINDS OF AID

Financial aid can be a grant that you keep, a wage that you earn, or a loan that you must repay. Grants, of course, are best. But almost every aid package offered to a student will include a combination of grants and loans with perhaps a job tossed in.

Aid can come from the government, from the college, or from other sources. Some will come because you ask for it. Some you'll find only if you look. Some aid will come directly to you. Some will go to you through your college.

The process of putting all forms of financial aid together is called packaging. That's the job of the college financial aid office. You'll get a letter, usually with your acceptance notice about a week later, telling you what's in your package.

You may hear the term preferential, or differential, packaging. That's aid officials' jargon for giving one student a better deal than another. Many colleges candidly admit they do it. Others do it but don't say so. Regardless of what euphemisms are offered, all preferential packaging is based on a single motive: one student gets a better deal than another because a college wants one student more than another.

GOVERNMENT AID

The largest distributor of financial aid is and probably always will be the federal government. Its slice of the aid pie shrunk during the last 15 years as programs were cut and colleges began giving away more in tuition discounts. But still $3 of every $4 spent to help students through college comes from Washington.

The government has six major aid programs offering grants, loans, and subsidized jobs:

> **Your financial aid package may include grants, loans, a tuition discount, and work-study.**

Pell Grants

Pells were created to provide college access for low-income students and once did a good job of it. But they've fallen behind spiraling college costs. The average Pell Grant last year was $1,518, just $400 higher than ten years ago. That increase doesn't even keep pace with inflation.

The Pell still is the only aid guaranteed to every eligible student. When the government's computer informs you of your Expected Family Contribution, it will tell you if it's low enough to qualify for a Pell. If you're eligible, you get one. Its size will be determined by your Need.

The eligibility level and size of the grants is set each year by the amount of money Congress puts into the program. For the year ending June 30, 1995, grants ranged from $400 to $2,300. Pell Grants are paid directly to the college, which credits them to the student's account.

Supplemental Grants

You'll see them mentioned in brochures as SEOGs (pronounced SOGs), which stands for Supplemental Educational Opportunity

Grants. They're also designed for low-income students but, unlike Pells, they're in a category called campus-based aid. That means each college gets a lump sum of SEOG money to distribute at its discretion under government guidelines.

Many colleges give SEOGs only to their neediest Pell Grant recipients. Others save a little for students who don't qualify for a Pell but still have a high Need. SEOGs can range from $100 to $4,000 a year but most are between $500 and $1,000. The average grant last year was $559. Ten years ago, it was $573.

Work-Study

Anyone who attended college in the last twenty years knows this program as College Work-Study or CWS. The name was changed in 1992 to Federal Work-Study but it's still a form of working your way through college with government help.

Work-study also is campus-based. Each school gets a lump sum from the government to pay 75 percent of a student's wages at campus or community jobs. The jobs are arranged by the college financial aid office and assigned as part of the student's aid package. Each job must pay at least the minimum wage.

> If you qualify for a Perkins Loan you can borrow up to $3,000 a year at 5% interest.

Work-study wages are paid directly to you to cover whatever expenses you desire. You can use the money for laundry, toothpaste, or air fare home. Last year, the average work-study student earned $1,066.

Perkins Loans

As they say about the Rose Bowl, it's the granddaddy of them all. It was born under another name—National Defense Education Loans—in 1958 when the government looked for ways to encourage kids to go to college and study science so we could match the Soviets' feat of orbiting a satellite.

Perkins is a campus-based loan program. Colleges get government money, which they loan to students who have Need. As loans are repaid the money is recirculated into new loans. Some colleges don't participate because of the time, effort, and paperwork that's required.

An advantage of a Perkins is its 5 percent interest. You need not start paying until nine months after you leave college. An undergraduate can borrow $3,000 a year up to a maximum of $15,000 for five years. The average Perkins Loan last year was $1,334.

Government rules say Perkins Loans should go to students with exceptional need and then allow each college to define "exceptional." As a rule, the higher your Need the more likely you'll be offered a Perkins.

The maximum a freshman can borrow with a Stafford is $2,625, at 8.2% or less interest.

Subsidized Stafford Loans

Your parents may fondly remember the Guaranteed Student Loans, or GSLs, which helped many of their generation get a degree. Here they are, dressed in new clothes with a new name.

A Subsidized Stafford typically is the cap on an aid package. The financial aid office goes as far as it feels it can with other help: grants, work-study jobs, Perkins Loans, tuition discounts. If your aid package still is less than your Need, you get a chance to apply for a Stafford.

There are limits. As a dependent student, you can borrow up to $2,625 as a freshman, $3,500 as a sophomore, $5,500 as a junior or senior. The interest rate is adjusted every June but can go no higher than 8.25 percent. For the year ending June 30, 1995, the rate was 7.43 percent.

Unlike Perkins, where the money is borrowed from the government through the college, Stafford Loans come from a bank. No credit or collateral is required. All you must have is a Need and a certificate from a college saying you're a student.

It's called a Subsidized Stafford because the government pays the interest while you're in college. Six months after you leave college, you must start repayment.

Unsubsidized Stafford Loans

A few pages ago, I said some aid is available for everyone. This is it. No Need is required.

The Unsubsidized Stafford is the new kid on the aid block, born in 1993 as Congress tried to help its middle-income constituents squeezed by soaring tuition costs.

It has the same interest rate, repayment schedule, and maximum loans as its subsidized sibling. But there is no subsidy. That means you're responsible for the interest while you're in college. You have the choice of paying it as a student or letting it ride and be added to the principal you need to start repaying when you leave school.

FFEL

You may hear or read about FFELs in discussions or literature on financial aid. FFEL stands for Federal Family Education Loans. It's a new term introduced by the government in 1995 to describe the Stafford Loan program. The Staffords officially are known as FFEL Stafford Loans. FFEL and Stafford can be, and are being, used interchangeably.

Direct Loans

This is a Stafford Loan with a new twist. Instead of borrowing from a bank, you borrow directly from the college, which gets the money from the government. Eligibility requirements are identical to the Stafford for subsidized or unsubsidized loans.

Direct loans were first tested at a handful of colleges in 1994, and more are joining the program each year. You can get a direct loan only if your college participates.

Other Washington Programs

Over the years, Congress has created other aid programs targeted to specific needs or certain groups of students. Here's a look at some of them:

- *PLUS Loans.* Another no-Needer. PLUS stands for Parent Loans for Undergraduate Students and that's what they are. Your parent may borrow at below-market interest any amount between the cost of your college and the total of your aid package. Need is not a requirement.
- *Byrd Scholarships.* Grants of $1,500 a year to outstanding high school graduates renewable for four years.
- *Paul Douglas Teacher Scholarships.* Grants of $5,000 a year renewable for four years, to outstanding high school graduates who plan to teach in elementary or secondary schools.
- *National Science Scholars.* Grants to encourage outstanding high school seniors to study math, science, or engineering. Maximum is $5,000, renewable for four years.

The Byrd, Douglas, and National Science grants are awarded by state scholarship agencies. Your counselor should know how to contact your state's agencies for eligibility and application information.

PRIVATE AID

Uncounted millions are available every year from service clubs, corporations, foundations, labor unions, and other philanthropic organizations. They're uncounted because no one knows how many there are. Directories publish lists of thousands but they admit up front that they don't include them all.

Much of the private scholarship money is restricted. It could be ticketed for students of certain religious faiths or ethnic heritage, to children of military veterans or union members, to Eagle Scouts or lacrosse players or journalism majors or females who want to be pharmacists.

You have to look for the money. A good place to start is your public library or counseling center, which should have a directory of scholarships and their eligibility requirements. An easier search tool is one of several commercial software programs, marketed to high schools and libraries, that allows you to enter a personal profile, then churns out a list of scholarships for which you might qualify.

But be aware that some colleges deduct the amount of private scholarships you win from the financial aid they give you. Some let you go for as much private money as you can find without penalty. Still other colleges deduct just certain types of scholarships. During your campus visits, ask each college about its policy.

INSTITUTIONAL AID

Institutional aid is a generic term covering all help offered by a college from its own resources. Last year, The College Board reports, it topped $8 billion nationally. Most of it comes in discounts off the published sticker price.

Tuition discounts are most often available from high-priced private schools.

Discounts are most prevalent at private colleges where the tuition is high. To stay competitive and keep their dorms full, they must help many students meet their costs while taking the full tuition from those who can afford it. Institutional aid is almost nonexistent at public universities or smaller state colleges where tuition is low. Some are prohibited by their state laws from discounting tuition.

A college giving away its money makes its own rules. That's why some colleges want more information than provided on the government's financial aid application. For the last few years, several hundred colleges used a supplemental form called the FAF (for Financial Aid Form). Many used it to get parents' home equity, which the government form doesn't ask. Others use supplement forms to get information from the noncustodial parent in a divorce or a family's assets from applicants who did not have to provide them because they qualified for a single needs test.

By the time you read this, the FAF likely will be history. It's being replaced by the new Financial Aid PROFILE described earlier in this chapter, for students entering college in September 1996.

THE GAPS

Most colleges try to meet all your Need with their financial aid package, but many fail. If your Need is, say, $9,000 and your aid totals $6,000, you've been "gapped." That's jargon that means your aid falls short of your need.

Colleges create gaps because they run out of money. State colleges with no cash of their own to give away spread their government aid to as many students as they can until it's gone.

Better students get a higher percentage of grants and discounts; others are offered more loans.

But they often can't meet a student's full Need. At private colleges, financial aid directors have a budget that limits the amount of tuition they can discount. It often gets spent before all Need is met.

Even colleges that claim they meet all students' Need—that no students are gapped—can define Need in many ways. They can use the Expected Family Contribution from the government formula or come up with their own modified EFC to calculate a lesser Need.

When private colleges don't have enough money for everyone, they distribute their institutional aid to meet their schools' priorities, encouraging certain students to enroll with generosity, discouraging others with gaps. Even at very selective colleges, the admission office may admit three times as many students as it needs for its freshman class because history shows only one third of those accepted will enroll. The financial aid office then uses its resources to attract the most desirable one third.

Colleges that have the funds to meet all students' Need and leave no gaps can adjust the aid packages to reflect their priorities. The better students get a higher percentage of grants and discounts; others are offered more loans. That's preferential packaging.

If you are gapped by a school that has money to give, it's sending the message: "Sorry, you are not a high priority. If you want to come here, you better find the money someplace else."

But remember the difference. Schools that don't give away their own money, like almost all public universities and state colleges, award all aid strictly on Need. If a gap exists, it's because the government money is gone. At schools that offer discounts, usually private colleges, a gap indicates priorities in student selection.

WHAT DOES ALL THIS MEAN?

You just had a crash course on the financial aid process. What have you learned to decide if First U., Second College, Third Tech, or Nearby State is the place to enroll?

Let's go back to the end of eleventh grade and see how your new knowledge can help. When you set up those campus visits, your second call (after the admission office) was to the financial aid office. You made appointments with financial aid people at each college. When you arrived, you talked to them about their application process and the supplemental forms they would need. You asked about their total cost of attendance and got dollar figures.

You offered a brief summary of your parents' financial condition. All responded that you had a good chance of getting some financial aid at their schools. You were friendly and eager to gain information. When you didn't understand something, you asked for an explanation in simple terms. The aid officer liked that.

Most students ignore the college financial aid office until they get an award letter. Then, after a phone call expressing chagrin that the aid package isn't larger, they forget about it and move on to more interesting pursuits.

You're not like most students. You have met someone in the aid office who knows your name, your face, and something about you. After your visits, the aid officers should be high on your list of people getting thank-you notes. Tell them how much you appreciated their advice and what a big help they were. Aid officers are among the most isolated people on campus. They value the few kind words they receive.

And when you call with a question about your aid package, won't you feel more comfortable if you know the person on the other end of the line? And if you know that person knows you?

In October of your senior year, when you were deciding which schools would get your application, you used the simple calculations described earlier in this chapter to figure your Estimated Family Contribution (EFC). You came up with ballpark numbers of $6,000 for your parents and $1,000 for yourself, for a total EFC of $7,000.

(If your older brother were still in college, your parents' contribution would be split in half, to $3,000, and your total EFC would be $4,000. But, alas, he's not.)

You figure that's fine, so far. If that's all you have to pay, you and your parents can scrape up $7,000. But the cost of attending First U. is $21,880; at Second College, it's $17,540; at Third Tech, it's $13,800. That means you'll have a financial Need ranging from about $14,000 at First U. to $6,800 at Third Tech. At Nearby State, the cost is $7,621. You can handle that without aid, and that's one of its attractions.

You mailed those applications, complete with essays and teacher and counselor recommendations, in mid-December. Most didn't have to be in that early. But Choosy U. had a January 15 deadline and you didn't want to get busy over the holidays and forget something. So while you did one, you did all.

At your counseling center, you got a copy of the Free Application for Federal Student Aid (known universally as FAFSA), the government form that triggers all aid programs. Now, the holiday season is here. It's one of those leisurely do-nothing days of the last week in December—it's time to take the FAFSA out of the drawer and get to work.

Why now? Because the law says the FAFSA cannot be filed until after January 1 of the year in which you're requesting aid. On the morning of January 2, the early birds will be at their post offices with their FAFSAs. Join the early birds. All financial aid is limited; most colleges eventually run out of money. It would be devastating to be accepted at First U., qualify for $14,000 in aid, and not get it because no money was left.

The FAFSA is an easy-to-understand four-page document that requires little work beyond digging out the records that you and your parents will need in April for taxes. If you're not sure about some of the numbers it wants, give it your best guess. That's perfectly legal. If your guess is wrong, you'll have a chance to amend it. Be sure *every* question is answered. If the answer is zero, write '0.' An unanswered question can produce a computer's request for more information that can delay your application a month. And be sure to sign it. A signature is easily overlooked be-

> **The FAFSA, the government aid form, can't be filed until after January 1; so do it January 2.**

cause, through some bureaucrat's whim, it's requested at the upper-left corner of the last page. More FAFSAs are returned to sender for a signature than for any other reason.

On January 2, after mailing your FAFSA, you can relax. Remember, you only send the FAFSA once. The information goes to every school you listed at the proper place on the form.

YOUR EFC

In the first week of February, a letter comes from the agency that processed your application. If you forgot to answer a question, it will be a request for more information. You'll have to provide the information and wait four more weeks for some news.

But you were diligent. You answered everything and signed your name. You open the letter and find a clump of blue papers. Across the top of the first one, it says Student Aid Report. It's a report from the computer that analyzed your financial Need. And there in the upper-right corner is word you've been awaiting: your Estimated Family Contribution is $7,290. Whew! Your ballpark calculations were pretty close. Only $290 off. You can live with that.

The Student Aid Report (SAR to acronym lovers) goes on in interminable bureaucratese to say you're not eligible for a Pell Grant (you already figured that) and then regurgitates all the data on your FAFSA. This is your chance to correct any bad guesses. If you have more accurate numbers than when you filled out the form, print them in the boxes provided and return the SAR, after making a copy for your records, of course. (If your parents' income was low enough to qualify for a Pell, the SAR would tell you the size of your grant. That would be a foundation on which a college would build your aid package.)

Now you go back to waiting. When the good news comes that four of your five schools accepted you, the costs are still unclear. You haven't heard about financial aid.

YOUR AID PACKAGES

Nearby State, the first to accept you, informs you in early March that it can't provide any direct aid but offers you the opportunity to borrow your $331 financial Need in a Subsidized Stafford Loan. (The $331 is Nearby's $7,621 cost minus your $7,290 EFC). Based on your ballpark calculation, you expected nothing from Nearby and that's what you got.

Your first real aid package comes from Third Tech, a week after it accepted you in mid-March. It totals $6,425. That's not too bad, you think. Third Tech's cost is $13,800. Your contribution is $7,290. That makes your Need $6,510. Third Tech is $85 short of covering it. You've been "gapped" by $85.

You look at the breakdown in the award letter. Third Tech's package includes an $800 work-study job, a $2,625 Subsidized Stafford Loan, and a $3,000 "institutional grant." That last item means a $3,000 discount.

You feel you've made it. Third Tech's deal will do it. You now know you can go to one of your top three choices by working a little, borrowing a little, and paying about $7,400. Not ideal, but manageable. You can forget Nearby State's safety valve.

In April, three days after your acceptance notice, comes the aid package from Second College. Your spirits drop. The cost at Second is $17,450, leaving you a Need of $10,160. But its offer totals only $9,625. That's more than $1,500 short of your Need.

After careful review, Second's package looks even worse. It asks you to take two loans, a Stafford and a Perkins, and earn $1,100 at a work-study job. Second College offers $3,000 of its own money, the same as Third Tech where the cost is less. And your feelings are a little wounded because Second has "gapped" you by $1,500. You know from your crash course above that means it found students it wants more than you.

To go to Second College, you would have to pay more, borrow more, and work for more than at Third Tech. Second and Third, in your opinion, are equally attractive colleges. The aid packages make Third a clear winner. But your top choice is still out. You pace a little wondering what First U. has in store.

Four days later, you find out. First U.'s award letter arrives and you whoop in delight. First is most expensive of the three at $21,880. Your Need there is the greatest, $14,590. And there it is, black numbers on white paper that say your aid totals $14,590. No gap.

You calm down from your euphoria to check the details. Hmmmm. A $1,000 work-study job. A $2,800 Perkins Loan. A $2,625 Subsidized Stafford. An institutional grant of $8,165. It could be better, but not bad. First U. is asking you to borrow $5,400 and work for $1,000 in exchange for an $8,100 discount. And Mom and Dad will pay only the $7,290 they've been counting on since they learned your EFC. Your first choice obviously wants you, too.

Your immediate inclination is to sign on the line accepting First U.'s offer and send it back in tomorrow's mail. But wait. You've been acting deliberately and rationally since you started this process three years ago and this is no time to start reacting from emotion. You decide to take a day or two to think about it. You pull out a yellow legal pad and list all three packages side by side, as shown on the table below:

First U. is the only one that meets your full Need, but Third Tech comes close. First U. offers you $5,100 more of its own money than Third Tech but it's $8,000 more expensive. You would have to borrow $5,425 to go to First U., $4,125 at Second College, only $2,625 at Third Tech.

You talk to Mom and Dad, who know something about borrowing. They have loans on a house and two cars. Would it be wise, you wonder, to take on a $5,400 debt as a freshman and perhaps that much again each of the next three years? That's about $22,000 to repay after college.

Dad's pretty good with a calculator. He starts punching buttons to figure what you would pay, based on each loan program's current

COMPARING AID PACKAGES

	First U.	Second College	Third Tech
Total Cost	$21,880	$17,450	$13,800
Your EFC	7,290	7,290	7,290
Your Need	14,590	10,160	6,510
Work-Study	1,000	1,100	800
Perkins Loan	2,800	1,500	
Stafford Loan	2,625	2,625	2,625
College grant	8,165	3,000	3,000
Total Aid	14,590	9,625	6,425

interest rates, on a $22,000 debt. His best estimate is you'll have payments of $270 a month if you take the full ten allowed years to repay. If you choose Third Tech, your debt and monthly payment would be about half that. That's a difference of $130 a month, over ten years, between First U. and Third Tech. (Second College you've forgotten. It would cost $1,500 a year more than the other two while you're a student.)

You think about First U. and Third Tech, your visits there, the people you met. You like both schools. But you really like First U. It's a place you know you can be comfortable and have fun while you're learning to become a science teacher. You like the idea that First U. considers you an attractive candidate because it's the only school that did not leave a gap. It's without a doubt your best fit.

Is it worth $130 of your monthly science teacher's pay to go to First U? You think about that for a few minutes. Then you answer your own question. You pick up First U's offer and sign your name.

BECOMING A PRIORITY

First U. met your full Need. Second College and Third Tech did not. First U. obviously was more interested in enticing you to its campus. You'll never know why you were more attractive at one college than another unless you ask the First U. admission staff.

At most colleges, the highest priorities go to students who couple excellent academic records with examples of leadership and special talent. But in some cases, you become a priority by sheer good luck.

That's what we'll look at in the next chapter. Luck.

MAYBE YOU'RE NOT A KID

If you are older than 24, even if you are still living with parents, you are independent for financial aid purposes. That means your parents' money doesn't count in figuring your Need.

If you use the worksheet to estimate your Expected Family Contribution, you can ignore the first part that asks for parents' income and assets. You can start down near the bottom at "Student's Contribution." The only numbers you'll need will be your own.

If you're married, your own numbers include your spouse's numbers. His income and assets must be added to yours. That's often called a marriage penalty. Your eligibility for aid decreases at marriage if your spouse has any income.

As an independent student, you can borrow more in the Stafford Loan program. Your loan limits are $6,625 as a freshman, $7,500 as a sophomore, $10,500 as a junior or senior.

CHAPTER NINE

MAKING YOUR OWN LUCK

. . . and using some of the luck you were born with

Somebody once said he'd rather be lucky than good. Being good certainly is better for your prospects of getting into college but, let's face it, some good old-fashioned luck doesn't hurt, either.

Luck comes in many shapes and sizes. For admission to a college, you can make your luck, you can fall into it, and you can be born with a little. Some is just a matter of being in the right place at the right time.

The more selective the college to which you're applying, the greater chance of luck coming into play. At an open admission state college that takes anyone with a high school diploma, luck's not an issue. You either have a diploma and are accepted or you don't and you're not. At the high-prestige colleges that accept about one third of their applicants, decisions become more subjective and luck often rears its head.

If you are a tuba player and apply the year the college band is short of tuba players, you have a fine chance of being accepted. By the time your application reaches the admission office, it will know about the pending tuba player shortage and will have received pleas from the music department to do something about it. If you apply a year later, when there are three tuba players in the freshman class, that bit of luck is gone.

SPECIAL PEOPLE

Admission officers, of course, don't talk about luck. In their jargon, lucky people are "special." When you hear the word "special" in an admission office or read it in college literature, you know that some people are getting lucky.

The word is most often used in one of two contexts: special talent or special consideration. Students with special talents usually get bonus points in their admission office score. The number of points varies with how desirable the talent is on that campus that year.

Special considerations for minorities and "legacies" are more prevalent than the directories indicate.

The special talent could be musical, it could be dramatic, it could be the ability to put a round ball through a hoop from beyond the three-point line. It could be something as simple as a desire to major in physics when the physics faculty is clamoring for more majors.

"Special consideration" usually refers to a group of students who get lucky. In those thick directories that you perused to start the college-selection process, you may have noticed some schools say "special consideration is given to . . ." The sentence most often ends with the word "minorities." Occasionally it says "minorities and children of alumni." Both special considerations are much more prevalent than the directories indicate.

Special consideration usually means an application is removed from the piles of regular applications and placed in a pile for members of its own specially considered group. Minorities thus are considered in competition only with other minorities.

Alumni kids, called legacies in admission office jargon, compete with others whose parents attended the college. Tuba players, if considered special, compete with other tuba players.

When you applied to Choosy U. in Chapter Seven, you felt it was a reach. You were less confident about being admitted to Choosy than to your other four selections but thought you should give it a shot. As it turned out, you just missed the last cut as evidenced by your spot on the Wait List.

Suppose Mom went to Choosy U. If she were as diligent as some parents, she might have written to the admission office or alumni office with the news that her daughter was applying, just so they would know. But that would be unnecessary. On page 2 of your application, you are asked the colleges your parents attended. If either Mom or Dad went to Choosy U., you become a legacy.

Choosy U.'s procedure, typical of more selective colleges, is to send all legacy applicants to the alumni office for an evaluation of the legacy factor. The dean of admission wants to know how important it is to the alumni director, whose main role is raising money, that each legacy be admitted.

The Choosy U. alumni office rates each applicant on a 1-to-4 scale based on the parent's generosity during fund-raising campaigns. A four goes to an alum who gives thousands every time he is asked. (Each college, of course, has its own rating system.)

Your Mom over the years regularly sends checks in the $200-to-$500 range to Choosy U. in response to Choosy's appeals. Your application returns to the admission office with a legacy rating of two. That's now considered in the mix with your others credentials: your high school record, your activities, your essay, your teacher recommendations. Since you just missed being accepted without it, a legacy rating of two gets you off the Wait List and into Choosy U.'s freshman class.

Did Mom buy you a place at Choosy? That's one way of looking at it. Worth David, Yale's retired admission dean, once put it another way: "Yale's family includes everyone from the newest freshman to the oldest alumnus. We take care of our family."

Penn's Dean Willis Stetson says "at a private institution our alumni and alumnae are our taxpayers."

From either perspective, it was luck you were born with. It can be big luck. A *USA TODAY* survey in 1992 found large differences in admission rates between legacies and other students. For example, Haverford reported accepting 86 percent of legacies, 43 percent of everyone else. At Penn, it was 73 percent to 47 percent. Notre Dame says 25 percent of each class is reserved for legacies.

Let's look at some other ways you can get lucky.

MINORITIES

For reasons well-documented by social scientists, some minorities are not represented on some campuses in proportion to their presence in the population. In admission offices, they're called underrepresented minorities. On campuses where the student body is predominantly white, that term usually includes African-Americans, Hispanics, and Native Americans.

Most predominantly white colleges have admission policies that give underrepresented minorities a break.

To correct this imbalance, most predominantly white colleges have admission policies that give underrepresented minorities a break. The dean of admission may have a goal, set by the college president or board of trustees, to raise the minority percentage of students to a certain level by a certain year. To meet the goal she must make sure a certain number of minorities are in each freshman class.

The dean has history working against her. Historically, a smaller percentage of minorities accept offers from predominantly white colleges than do white students. The dean knows that if she accepts 1,000 white students 500 will enroll, but from 1,000 African-Americans she'll get about 280 freshmen. (Enrollment rates differ for each college.)

That's why underrepresented minorities are often in a special pool, competing only with each other. That's why acceptance letters go to a higher percentage of minorities than whites. That's why, at least for getting into college, being an underrepresented minority is luck you were born with.

GENDER

You don't think it matters which sex you were born into, unless you're looking at a single-sex college. It usually doesn't, but it can.

Most admission offices strive for a gender balance. Suppose Choosy U. has guidelines that aim for a gender split no greater than 52 percent to 48 percent in each freshman class. Suppose the admission staff, as it's making its final decision, realizes it has accepted too many men. It must quickly take more women, and probably drop some men, to keep the balance. This has been known to happen. If you're female, your sex may get you into Choosy U. That's luck you'll never know you had. But some gender-based luck is available for the taking.

Females majoring in engineering get points for being female even at the most selective colleges.

A college that recently switched from single-sex to coed, and several have done so, still has a large majority of one gender. It's likely to be actively recruiting students of the sex that once was excluded, trying to spread the word that they're now welcome. Applicants of the minority sex, male or female, get a definite break.

Gender-based advantages also exist for students interested in fields where their sex traditionally has been outnumbered.

Females majoring in engineering, for example, get points for being female even at the most selective colleges. MIT accepts 28 percent of its male applicants versus 48 percent of its female applicants. Caltech takes 24 percent of the men who apply, 36 percent of the women. Males who'd like to be nurses or teachers get similar breaks.

TALENT

Now we start talking about luck you have earned, not an accident of birth. If you have developed any type of special talent by the time you apply to college, a college somewhere is looking for it and will give you an edge because you have it.

The obvious talents that make students attractive to colleges are music, drama, and athletics. The jocks are in a category by themselves. Their high school coaches keep them well-apprised of which colleges are interested in their level of talent. If a recruited athlete meets a college's minimum academic standards—at some colleges the minimum is lowered if necessary—the admission office affixes its rubber stamp. Even the 8 Ivy League schools give a coach's priority list heavy weight in the admission decisions, so long as minimum academic standards are met.

> **The obvious talents that make students attractive to colleges are music, drama, and athletics.**

Musicians and thespians aren't as actively recruited as athletes but their talents are just as desirable to faculty in their fields. But they must seek out colleges that desire their talents.

If you play a musical instrument make a tape of some of your better efforts. Before your campus visit, call or write the music department with the news that you will be visiting the college as a potential applicant, and that you would like to chat about its band and orchestra and drop off a tape. Almost any music director will welcome you. Even if you don't plan to major in music your talent could be needed for football halftime shows.

If the music director likes what he hears on your tape he'll send a note to the admission office. You'll have a definite edge. At some colleges a faculty recommendation gets almost as much weight as a request from a coach. You will have made your own luck.

The same luck-building recipe works if you're a decent actress, a competent school newspaper editor, or just a fine math, chemistry, physics, or foreign language student. If you have examples of work in which you take pride—which means you have a special talent—make an effort to share them with someone in the appropriate college faculty department. If you intend to major in that field, so much the better.

A fact of academic life on every campus is that faculty departments covet students who major in their fields. Without enough students, they can't justify their existence to administrators who prepare budgets. If you have a talent in a certain field and can impress a professor with it, the professor is likely to send that all-important note to the admission office. You're making your luck.

Good teachers and counselors can help make your luck, too. A high school band director who knows Distant U. is running short of tubas can advise his senior tuba player to look at Distant U., with a pretty good chance that she'll be accepted.

Counselors in regular communication with college admission offices—and the good ones are—know where the physics department and Romance language faculty need students. In some cases, when a small faculty department complains about a lack of students, the admission office sends it all the applicants who intend to major in that field and lets the faculty pick who it wants.

GEOGRAPHY

When Richard Steele was dean of admission at Duke, he once exhibited a frustration common in his business by saying: "If a kid from North Dakota walked into my office today, I'd admit him on the spot."

Steele exaggerated to make a valid point. Admission officers feel pressure, from their presidents and others who set policy, to diversify their student bodies with more than ethnic minorities. Many colleges like a wide geographic representation. Some colleges would love to send out brochures saying they have students from all 50 states. But they're foiled because that darn admission office can't find anyone from North Dakota.

If you don't mind traveling, you can find some built-in luck by looking at colleges where few people from your area apply. A student from Montana has a better chance of getting into Harvard than a student from New York with identical academic credentials. The Harvard admission staff won't volunteer this information but, displaying the honesty one expects from Harvard, will tell you it's true if you ask.

With a few exceptions, however, the geography edge works only at private colleges. Almost all state schools cater to their state's residents who pay the taxes that subsidize them. One exception is the University of Vermont, which actively recruits out-of-staters and seeks geographic diversity.

The University of North Carolina, for one, is required by state law to have a certain percentage of its students from North Carolina. The popularity among students across the country of North Carolina's flagship campus at Chapel Hill makes its out-of-state admission process the nation's most selective. UNC–Chapel Hill accepts almost half the North Carolinians who apply but only 13 percent of the out-of-staters. That's a tougher ticket than Harvard, which takes 16 percent of its applicants.

> **You can find some built-in luck by looking at private colleges where few people from your area apply.**

That takes us back to the enormous luck of legacies. At UNC–Chapel Hill, children of alumni are treated as North Carolina residents for admission purposes regardless of where they live.

BACKGROUND

If you're the first person in your family to go to college, you have some built-in luck at many selective admission offices. That's because you'll add some diversity.

Socioeconomic diversity is as welcome as the other kinds. A student from a blue-collar background, or from a family in which higher education is not a tradition, brings an experience not typical to many campuses. That difference gives you an edge just as life experience provides an advantage to the older student.

Any experience in your background that differs from the majority of the student body scores points in an admission office and could tip the scale in your favor on a close call. It could be the difference between Wait List and freshman class. Such experiences could be having lived in another country, research work in a college lab, home schooling, or employment in an unusual occupation.

Finally, your high school could be lucky. If a college admission office knows your school and knows that students who come from it do well, you have an advantage.

The bottom-line question a Choosy U. admission officer must answer is: Will this student be able to handle Choosy U.'s work?

If 90 percent of the students from your school have been successful at Choosy U., that's evidence that others who come from your school also can do it. That's a little bit of luck for you.

CHAPTER TEN

THE TWO-YEAR OPTION

. . . a convenient, inexpensive head start

I didn't forget. If you're considering a two-year college as one of your options or happen to know one of the 6.4 million students now attending a two-year school, you might be wondering why I have ignored the nation's most popular form of higher education.

You could say I was saving the best for last. In some respects, you're right. For many students—6.4 million of you can't be wrong—a two-year college is the best choice.

If it's the best fit for you, that's where you should enroll. Almost half (49 percent) of U.S. college students take their first higher education course on a two-year campus.

It's certainly best in cost. Average tuition at public two-year colleges is half the average at four-year public campuses and one tenth the average at private colleges.

It's usually the most convenient. Except in our most rural areas, a two-year college exists within an easy drive of every U.S. resident. In some states every county has at least one.

It frequently gives the best individual attention to a student's specific needs. Two-year colleges, as they have evolved over the years, fill many roles. They typically offer a wider menu of education choices than their four-year brethren. Most have become all-purpose educational institutions, providing whatever service is demanded by their customers—the students of their communities.

They exist to offer folks in their communities:

- An easy, inexpensive start toward a four-year college degree.
- A place to acquire a skill, such as computer repair, nursing, graphic design, dental hygiene, accounting, robotics, physical therapy, or cosmetology, to name just a few.

Two-year colleges also call themselves many things. Most now identify themselves as community colleges. Some, including those like Cottey College in Missouri that do not serve a single community, use the older term: junior college. Many, particularly in the South, say they are technical colleges.

The American Association of Junior Colleges, formed in the 1940s, changed its name to the American Association of Community and Junior Colleges as the "community college" concept became popular. Recently, it thought about becoming the American Association of Community, Junior, and Technical Colleges but dropped that as a bad idea. More recently, in 1993,

GROWTH IN TWO-YEAR COLLEGES

Enrollment in two-year colleges has grown considerably since 1945.

1945	294,000
1955	765,000
1965	1,292,000
1975	4,063,000
1980	4,825,000
1985	4,980,000
1990	5,851,000
1992	6,554,000

Source: American Association of Community Colleges

it again renamed itself simply the American Association of Community Colleges. But junior and technical colleges still are welcome as members.

Regardless of the name, all these institutions come together in the mission of offering students their first two years of post–high school education. All offer the associate degree, which can be earned in two years.

Another form of two-year college is the proprietary school, which is in business to make a profit by teaching a skill such as hair styling or refrigerator repair. Those schools are strictly business and like businesses in all fields, some are credible and some are not. If you're considering such a school, check it out with other customers and the Better Business Bureau, just as you would any business.

A vast majority of two-year colleges (1,291 of the 1,472) are public, operated by state, county, or municipal governments. And these public schools have 97 percent of the nation's two-year students. For that reason, while recognizing that private two-year colleges exist as alternatives to the four-year private sector, the rest of this chapter will discuss the public schools.

POPULARITY

The two-year colleges are the fastest-growing segment of education at any level, kindergarten through graduate school. Their 6.4 million students are a 5 percent increase over 1991 and a 35 percent jump since 1981.

Their popularity is attributed to the three factors mentioned above: cost, convenience, and variety of curriculum. Those factors also produce a student body well mixed in terms of age, race, and educational goal. Almost one third (31 percent) of students at two-year colleges are over 30.

And two-year colleges have few entrance barriers. Some have specific requirements for certain programs such as nursing, but for most fields they are open admission schools taking anyone with a high school diploma or its equivalent. The only restrictions come at places like Miami-Dade Community College in Florida, where the demand exceeds the supply and enrollment must be capped when facilities are taxed to capacity. Even those schools aren't selective. It's first come, first admitted. Most do, however, have minimum academic standards for students who want to stay. You can flunk out of a two-year college as easily as anywhere else.

Cost

The average tuition for a full-time student at a two-year college in 1994–95 was $1,298. At a four-year public college, it was $2,686. At four-year private colleges, tuition averaged $11,007. Those figures are *not* tuition, room and board, or cost of attendance, or any of the other dollar totals cited in earlier chapters. They represent tuition, and only tuition, because it's the only significant expense at a two-year college. Compared to the alternatives, it may be significant but it's hardly large.

Most two-year colleges are open admission schools: first come, first admitted.

Depending on where you live, the cost could be even lower. Average annual tuition at California community colleges is $390, in North Carolina it's $504, in Arizona $601, in Kentucky $817.

Catering to their large corps of part-time students, most two-year colleges offer the opportunity to pay by the course or by the credit hour. A student can move toward a degree at the rate of one or two courses per semester if education funds are tight.

Convenience

Two-year colleges have become, if not ubiquitous, certainly plentiful. In the last three decades, I have lived in seven states and never have been more than 30 minutes away from a two-year campus. Most Americans probably have one just as close. Transportation costs are a gallon of gas a day. That's convenience.

With very few exceptions, two-year colleges are not residential. They have no dorms. All students commute. This is an attraction to the part-timer, the adult, and anyone else who prefers to stay home while attending college and could feel out of place in a dorm-dominated environment.

Curriculum

A typical two-year college will split its curricular menu just about 50-50. Half the courses will be from the traditional academic mold—the sciences, humanities, arts, foreign languages—for the student preparing to move on to a bachelor's degree or more. The other half are for students who come to learn a skill, to move up on the employment ladder, to make a midlife career change.

The result is a student body melting pot. Adults blend easily with teenagers, premed students and music majors mix and share social lives with potential auto mechanics and dental technicians. And no one seems to notice the difference. Diversity is a fact of life, not a goal being sought by admission offices.

At most you can pay by the course or by the credit hour.

Diversity also is common among teaching staffs. A large segment of the faculty typically consists of people with real-world expertise hired part-time to share their knowledge with students. The hidebound traditions of the four-year-college world, where a Ph.D. and the ability to conduct research are greater assets for a professor than teaching his students, do not exist at two-year campuses. Teaching is the faculty's only job.

Many two-year colleges have agreements with four-year colleges in their states that ease the way for transfers between the institutions. They spell out, for example, what courses on the two-year campus are required, and accepted, in pursuit of a four-year degree. In some of the agreements, four-year schools guarantee admission to anyone completing a prescribed program at the two-year college.

GOOD OPTIONS FOR MANY

Forty years ago, two-year colleges (then known almost exclusively as junior colleges) were considered the college of last resort. They were the places to go if you couldn't make it anywhere else.

Over the decades, the stigma gradually has disappeared. Two-year campuses are viable, acceptable options for students without the time, money, inclination, or educational goal to attend a four-year institution. They are for many the college of *first* resort.

Everyone thinking about college should consider the two-year option. Many, for valid reasons, will consider it and quickly reject it. Others should give it a place on their lists as they search for the proper fit.

Let's return again to tenth grade when you started making lists. On that list of important factors that led to your first cut, along with size, location, and the rest, should be the two-year option. Given the advantages described above, could a two-year college be the right place for you to enter higher education? Could it be your best fit? Or one of the right fits?

About half the courses are academic, the other half skill-oriented.

WHO FITS?

Are you worried about cost? Do you have a strong desire to stay home and commute to college classes? Do you have a less-than-stellar high school academic record that leaves you wondering about your chances for admission? Are you often intimidated by people who act "smarter" than you?

Answer "yes" to any of those questions and the two-year option is worth serious thought.

Back in Chapter One, when we walked through that first list of fit-finding factors, we didn't include cost. I suggested you find the colleges that are right for you, then learn how much each will require you to pay. Nothing should be ruled out just because you think it's too expensive.

But when the time comes to make your decision, cost enters the equation. You weigh financial aid offers along with the other variables. If your finances are tight and cost will weigh heavily in your decision, a low-cost "safety valve" school should be on your list. It could be Nearby State. It could be Convenient Community College.

Don't exclude Choosy U. because of its $25,000 annual tab. You might get $23,500 in aid and pay only $1,500. But your most desirable backup if all else fails might well be Convenient CC.

Then there's the grade problem. After checking admission requirements at colleges that interest you, disappointment could set in. Perhaps they're looking for grade point averages and test scores and a class rank that you won't attain. You could have reached a 3.0 grade point average and made the top 20 percent of your class, but other things got in the way. Occasionally you didn't give those chemistry classes the attention they deserved.

If cost is a big issue in the end, Convenient CC may be your best fit.

Two-year colleges, more often than their public relations people like to admit, are used as proving grounds where students can wipe away a dismal high school record.

Admission officers at four-year colleges want to know how well you will handle college work. The best evidence you can offer is a record of handling it well. An "all-A" transcript from a two-year college quickly will overcome the negative impression produced by a string of C's in high school. Recommendations from professors at a two-year college, who gave you the A's, will carry more weight than letters from high school teachers who gave you lesser grades.

And perhaps you aren't ready to charge full speed into the rigors of college life. You would rather have a slow entry to gradually become acclimated to college work. In that case, the two-year option is ideal.

You can take one or two courses a year, maybe even holding a job at the same time, and transfer to a four-year institution when you feel you're ready. You'll be in good company. Two thirds of all two-year college students take less than a full-time course load.

FINANCIAL HELP

The rules for financial aid programs are the same regardless of what college you attend. The information from your FAFSA will be used the same way at Convenient Community College as it is at Choosy U.

The big difference, of course, will be your financial Need. Remember, your Need is determined by subtracting your expected family contribution from the college cost. At two-year colleges, the cost is so low that you could wind up with no Need, thus no eligibility for need-based aid. And public two-year colleges have no institutional money to give away.

Two-year colleges are used as proving grounds where students can wipe away a dismal high school record.

Still, 30 percent of two-year students receive some form of financial aid. If you're considering a two-year college, add its name to the list on your FAFSA. You could be surprised at the result.

MAYBE YOU'RE NOT A KID

The average age of a two-year-college student is 29. That fact alone tells you adults are not just welcome, they're abundant. The All-USA Academic Team for Two-Year Colleges, which honors outstanding students at the two-year level, annually has about half its members from the over-30 crowd. The two-year option is ideal for the adult who wants to learn a new skill, train for a new career, or just add to her knowledge.

If you're worried about a 15-year-old high school transcript, or afraid today's bright young things will outshine you, or fearful of being required to retake the SAT at your advanced age, the two-year option eliminates your concerns.

Like the underachieving high school graduate, you can use a two-year college as a proving ground to convince other colleges you can handle their work. And you can use it, too, for gradual reentry, building up slowly to a full-time college schedule.

Adults calling *USA TODAY*'s College Admission Hotline often get this advice from the four-year-college folks: "Start at a two-year college. Build an academic record and bring that record to us. If your record is good, we'll welcome you."

CHAPTER ELEVEN

THE EXPERTS SPEAK

. . . the questions you ask, the answers you receive

Is a "B" in an honors course worth more than an "A" in a regular course? Why is joining clubs important for getting into college? Does a bad credit rating hurt your chances for financial aid? Should you take the SAT more than once? If your older sister didn't get any aid, should you bother to apply?

Those are among more than 27,000 questions asked by *USA TODAY* readers since 1988 on the newspaper's annual College Admission and Financial Aid Hotline. Every October, financial aid and admission officers from campuses across the country are invited to *USA TODAY*'s Arlington, Va., headquarters. For three days, 12 hours a day, they answer calls from readers on a toll-free number appearing in newspapers.

Just about all of the questions handled in the seven years of hotlines are answered in detail elsewhere in this book. But to reinforce those points, we are printing a collection of the questions— typical and unusual—and the answers in the experts' own words right here. In some cases, more than one answer is provided to offer a perspective from different colleges. (The experts are identified by their institutions at the time they answered the questions, which may not be where they work now.)

Test Scores

Q. How important is the SAT in the college admission decision?

A-1. At most colleges, test scores are not as important as your high school academic record. Find the school you want to attend, then ask how much weight it gives to test scores.

—John Torpie, Clarkson University

A-2. High school grades are a much better indicator than test scores of how a student will do in college. A test score is merely a snapshot of one day in a student's life. We're more interested in what you've done during four years than for four hours on a Saturday morning.

—John Klockentager, Buena Vista College

A-3. We give the high school record 60 percent of the weight in our decisions. Activities get 20 percent and test scores 20 percent.

—James Walters, University of North Carolina-Chapel Hill

Q. Does my SAT score play an important part in my ability to get a scholarship?

A. Yes and no. An SAT score has no effect at all on need-based aid such as Pell Grants and Stafford Loans. But it is one piece of your application and the better your academic record, the better your chances of getting a merit scholarship. The SAT score will be weighted differently by every school.—*Marcelle Tyburski, Colgate University*

Q. As a high school sophomore, I receive conflicting advice on college entrance exams. I took the PSAT this October and plan to take it again next fall. Should I also take the SAT/ACT next year or wait until my senior year?

A. There is no reason to repeat the PSAT. You should take the SAT or ACT in the latter half of your junior year. I strongly counsel against waiting for the senior year. There's learning that occurs, some test-wisdom that you gain, simply by taking the exam. Then take it again as a senior. When you repeat, the average score increase is 40 points.

—Walters

Q. If I miss the PSAT, does that exclude me from the scholarship lists?

A. Missing the PSAT in tenth grade eliminates you from consideration for National Merit Scholarships. It has no effect on your eligibility for other financial aid or admission to college.—*Walters.*

Admission Criteria

Q. My son is an Eagle Scout. Will that help him get into college?

A. It should. Colleges look for a serious commitment to activities outside school. Gaining Eagle Scout rank certainly is evidence of a commitment.   —*Bill Davis, College of William & Mary*

Q. Why do you have a better chance of getting into college if you are involved in clubs or sports? I thought the point of going to college is to get an education.

A. Some colleges pay little attention to out-of-class activities. They're after scholars. We are a classic residential campus. We want students involved in this beautiful, alive place. We place 20 percent of the (application) weight on outside activities and leadership, with 60 percent on high school academic record, and 20 percent on test scores. We want students who will make contributions in activities.—*Walters*

Q. Will applying for financial aid hurt my daughter's chances of getting accepted by a college?

A. Most schools admit students on a need-blind basis, which means their financial condition isn't a factor. That means they'll accept you if you qualify academically. It doesn't necessarily mean they'll give you all the financial aid you need. A few selective schools use financial need as a factor in their admission decisions and marginal students who don't apply for aid have an edge. If an application asks if you are applying for financial aid, that's why.—*Jim Lyons, Seattle University*

Q. My daughter's application asks for her class rank. Her high school doesn't rank students. What should she do?

A. Don't leave it blank. Write a note explaining that your school doesn't use a ranking process. Don't leave anything unanswered. It will look like you don't care.—*Wendy Beckemeyer, Cottey College*

Q. What is the International Baccalaureate program worth for getting into college?

A. The IB, an international advanced curriculum, has great value in admission offices. They consider it equal to AP (Advanced Placement) and some rank it a notch or two higher. It's worth taking.

—Ron Poitier, Elizabethtown College

Q. How important is two years of foreign language in high school for college admission?

A. The best colleges are preparing future leaders of the global village. We want to see kids with an interest in understanding other cultures. The best indication of that in the high school curriculum is foreign language study.—*Gary Ripple, Lafayette College*

Q. Will home schooling hurt my children's chances of being accepted by a quality college?

A. You need to educate the college about what your children have learned. They should take the SAT or ACT and some achievement tests to show they are ready to do college work. Most colleges require an interview before admitting home-schooled students.

—Rich Edgar, St. Mary's College, Maryland

College Applications

Q. Should I apply to a college for early decision, which means I must commit to that school, or wait to see if I can get more financial aid somewhere else?

A. Ask your first-choice school for an early estimate of how much aid you're likely to get. Then if you can't afford that school you have time to apply to others where your aid package might be better.

—Patricia Farmer, St. Lawrence University

Q. I know I should schedule an on-campus interview. But what if I mess up?

A. Relax. The interviewer's job is to impress you. You are the customer. An interview is nothing more than an exchange of information.

—Jeff Grimm, U. of Pittsburgh–Bradford

High School Strength

Q. I've heard that colleges have an unpublished chart that assigns scores to high schools and those students who attend higher scoring schools are given an edge.

A-1. Colleges develop an understanding of competition that exists within a high school. We measure each student against the opportunities that his or her high school provides. Students who take full advantage of their opportunities have an edge over those who don't. Students from more competitive high schools are not at an automatic advantage.

—Ripple

A-2. We assign a 1-to-5 ranking of a high school's strength. We use the ranking subjectively as one element of the student's application. If a student has not been in a highly competitive situation, it could work against him. Clearly, a strong student won't get penalized because he's not in a strong school. But in a highly competitive school, we would go deeper into the class. *—Walters*

Q. Our high school is going to outcomes-based education, which means a pass-fail grading system instead of letter grades. How will that affect my children's chances of getting into a competitive college?

A. When we see students without standard measures of academic progress—home-schooling is an example—we rely more heavily on standardized tests such as the SAT, ACT, and Achievement Tests. And the onus is on the school to tell us how the student performs relative to the rest of his class. But if outcomes-based education spreads, colleges eventually will develop their own methods of assessing these students.*—Ron Moss, Southern Methodist University*

Financial Aid Eligibility

Q. What's the income cutoff for financial aid?

A. There is no income cutoff. We recommend all students apply for aid, at least for their first year. Many variables affect financial need and eligibility for aid and many schools have non-need-based aid.

—Robin Famiglietti, Eckerd College

Q. How much am I allowed to make before my income is deducted from my financial aid eligibility?

A. The first $1,750 a student earns each year is not considered in the financial need formula. A percentage of everything you earn over that is expected to pay for college.*—Beckemeyer*

Q. Is it possible for a person who has gone through bankruptcy to be eligible for financial aid?

A. Bankruptcies and poor credit ratings are not considered in determining financial need and eligibility for need-based aid, including subsidized student loans. But if you're in default of an earlier student loan, you are ineligible.—*Curtis Powell, Georgetown University*

Q. I'm in default on a student loan. How do I get out of that status?

A. Make six consecutive monthly payments on time and the loan agency is allowed to restore your eligibility. But it is not required to take you out of default. It may insist that you repay the entire loan.
                              —*William Mack, Rochester Institute of Technology*

Q. I was turned down for an education loan for my son because of a bad credit rating. But your hotline experts say the bank can't look at my credit history for student loans. Who's right?

A. A student's personal credit history is not considered except when a student has defaulted on a previous loan. But you're not a student. You were applying for a PLUS loan, available to parents, and banks can deny PLUS for bad credit records.—*Mack*

Q. If one parent is going to college, does it affect the Expected Family Contribution as calculated on the federal Student Aid Report?

A. Yes, a parent in college will reduce the Expected Family Contribution for every family member. The total family contribution is split evenly among each member enrolled in college for at least six credits.
                              —*Ron Shunk, Gettysburg College*

Q. My parents' home is paid for. Will that affect my eligibility for aid?

A. Home equity no longer is considered in calculating eligibility for government aid programs. But some colleges still look at it in awarding their own institutional grants.—*Famiglietti*

Q. Is it true that my child will be an independent for financial aid purposes (parents' income not counted) if I don't claim him as a dependent on my tax return for two years?

A. That was true a few years ago but the rules have changed. Now to be independent, a student must fit one of six categories: 24 or older, married, graduate student, military veteran, orphan or ward of a court, tax-deductible dependents.—*Barry McCarty, Lafayette College*

Q. Why won't my college count my brother who is in graduate school in determining my financial aid?

A. The number of dependent family members in college is a key factor in how much you're expected to pay. But graduate students are by law independents. Your brother can't be both at the same time.
—Mark Rizzieri, George Washington U.

Q. I'm a legal guardian for my niece. Her parents are alive but not involved in her care. Will my income be used for her financial aid eligibility?

A. No. Your niece under federal law is independent. Only her income and assets will be considered.*—Kathleen Wicks, Trinity (D.C.) College*

Q. Is it true that not all schools meet 100 percent of a student's financial need?

A. Yes. It depends on the institution and the amount of money it has available. These days, most institutions don't have enough to meet all students' full need. Those who apply earliest often get the best aid packages.*—Sheila Sauls-White, Capitol College*

Financial Aid Applications

Q. Do you have to send a financial aid form to every college you applied to before you know if you're accepted?

A. Every school has its own policy. We want an FAF (Financial Aid Form) at the same time as the application. Others want them separately. The instructions that come with your applications should tell you what to do. The application for federal aid (FAFSA) is submitted once, after January 1, and its information is sent to all schools on your list.*—Tyburski*

Q. Should parents accompany a student on a college visit?

A. Absolutely. Parents may have questions the student doesn't think of. It's important for parents to see the school, its surroundings, and how the student fits in.*—Susan Potter, Thomas College*

Q. What can I do to get off a college wait list?

A. Don't become a nuisance. Let the college admission office know—once—by phone call or letter that you're seriously interested. That helps because we prefer to admit people who will enroll. But don't bug them with phone calls every other day, because some exasperated staff member might make a note of it in your folder.*—Moss*

Q. Will it help or hurt to take a year off before college?

A. A year of maturing will help. It's a way to ask the most important question: Do I really want to go to college? No college will consider a year off a negative.—*Nancy Church, Sweet Briar College*

Q. How soon should I apply for (government) financial aid?

A. Apply no earlier than Jan. 1, and no later than Jan. 2 (if you want the best chances of getting aid). Almost all aid programs have limited funds. You could be eligible for all kinds of aid but by the time your application arrives, it's gone. If you snooze, you lose.
                                              —*Sarah Bauder, St. Mary's (Md.) College*

Q. I live alone in a house my parents bought. They moved back to Africa and they don't pay any of my bills. I have trouble getting financial aid because colleges think I live with them. Is there a way around this?

A. Take all the documentation you have, the bills you've paid and your receipts, to the financial aid office and explain your situation. They can use professional judgment to override the federal formula and declare you independent. But the burden of proof is on you.—*Powell*

Q. We own a small business and won't have our tax information until early April. If we estimate our finances on a financial aid application, can the application be amended later?

A. A month after you apply for aid, you'll get a Student Aid Report that gives you an opportunity to change the information you submitted. If you have amendments to make after that, send a copy of your tax return to the college financial aid office to show the changes.
                                                                                    —*Powell*

Q. My son, a sophomore, has been receiving all kinds of mail from colleges he never heard of. He hasn't sent away for anything. How are these colleges getting his name?

A. They bought it. When your son took the PSAT, his name, score, and demographic information went into a national database. Colleges buy mailing list of students who fit their profiles. The more mail you get, the more you are in demand. We only buy people who fit what we want.—*Andrew Weller, Marymount University, Virginia*

Q. How can I make my application essay work to my advantage?

A. Use the essay to reveal important personal characteristics that won't be found anywhere else in your application package. Think about how other students will answer the essay question, then do something else.—*Dennis Matthews, Oglethorpe University.*

Marriage Penalty

Q. I'm a single working mother with an annual income of $15,349. I have sole custody of my 16-year-old daughter. I plan to be married next summer at the end of my daughter's junior year. My fiancé does not intend to contribute to her college costs. How do we apply for financial aid without involving my new husband?

A. Sorry, when he marries you he's involved. A marriage penalty is built into the financial aid laws written by Congress. The only recourse for couples who don't like it is to complain to their Congressional members. The law requires custodial parents to report income and assets on a student's financial aid application even if one is a brand-new stepparent. If you just married someone who has a child, even if you didn't know that child a month ago, the law says you must contribute to the child's college costs.—*Barry McCarty, Lafayette College*

Q. I am married and making $70,000 a year. My stepdaughter is a high school sophomore. Her mother is on welfare. I have read my husband and I are better off getting divorced before my stepdaughter applies to college so she can get financial aid. Is that true?

A. I'd like to believe that marriages are built on more than posturing for financial aid. But if you separated, the father would not be reporting your income, and his daughter's financial need would be greater.
—McCarty

Saving for College/Scholarships

Q. I am planning to buy Series E savings bonds for my 1-year-old grandson's college education. Should the bonds be issued in the child's name or the father's name?

A. It's better to put them in the parent's name. Students' assets are considered about six times more harshly than parents' assets in the financial need formula. It would be even better to keep them in your own name. Grandparents' assets aren't considered at all.—*McCarty*

Q. Is a scholarship search service worth the money?

A. Only if you feel like paying someone to do something you can do for yourself. Most services produce lists of potential scholarships you can get from any decent directory or commercial software program, available in libraries and school guidance offices.—*Beckemeyer*

Q. I have 1-year-old twins. How much will I have to save to put them through school from 2012 to 2016?

A. Ivy League colleges just raised their tuitions about 5 percent. If tuitions go up at the same rate each year for 17 years, you'll need to save $500 per kid per month. In your case that's $12,000 a year. And make sure your broker gets you an 8 percent return on your investments.

—Jim Spencer, Lycoming College

Q. I gave my grandson, 12, stock now worth $8,000. It is registered in his name. Will this small net worth jeopardize his chance of getting a student loan?

A. It is a factor that's considered in determining financial need. A portion of it should be used for educational costs. That is only fair.—*McCarty*

Q. Must I report the money in my 401(k) and EE bonds on my daughter's financial aid form?

A. Yes, you must report your EE bonds. But the good news is that money stashed away in retirement accounts, such as a 401(k), does not have to be reported. You need only report the amount you contributed to the plan this year.—*McCarty.*

If You're Not A Kid

Q. I'm an older student interested in returning to school. Am I at a disadvantage competing with younger students?

A-1. No. Most colleges value older students because of what they add in diversity and life experience. And, frankly, most schools could not survive without nontraditional students. Visit the campus, talk to students and an admission officer to see if you're comfortable.—*Lyons.*

A-2. I say to adult students that you will not feel out of place on our campus. There will be enough of you that you will not feel odd or unusual. Adults are remarkably successful in college. They're a heckuva good bet. We give those students a decided break and I think that's true at most institutions in the country.—*Walters*

Q. I'm 31, a single parent with a 3.6 GPA at a community college. I'd like to transfer to a four-year women's college. Is it a good idea at my age?

A. Some women's colleges are geared to traditional-age students. Others have programs and support services such as child care and advice on housing for nontraditional students like you. Your first step should be to ask an admission office what support the college offers for older students.—*Craig Wesley, St. Norbert College*

Q. I'm 32 years old and run a dry-cleaning business. I enrolled in Miami-Dade Community College. I'm worried if I did the right thing.

A. You did exactly the right thing. Especially if you're apprehensive about fitting into the lifestyle of younger students at a four-year school where most students live on campus. Get your feet wet and build an academic record at a community college, then transfer.

—Claire MacDonald, University of Baltimore

Q. I didn't think about college while I was in high school. Now that I've been working awhile, I think I would like to try Ohio State. Would they take me?

A. With your high school record, your best bet is to enroll in your local community college. Take some remedial courses and build a record of college work. Get tested and evaluated and you'll have something to show the Ohio State people.—*W.G. Starling, Wake Forest University*

INDEX

Essential Guides for Today's College-Bound Student

Peterson's Guide to Four-Year Colleges 1996

Descriptions of over 2,000 colleges, providing guidance on selecting the right school, getting in, and financial aid. Includes CAP—College Application Planner, IBM -compatible software to help students select and apply to colleges.
ISBN 1-56079-481-X, 2,924 pp., 81/2 x 11, $19.95 pb, 26th edition

#1 Bestselling College Guide!

Paying Less for College 1996

"One of the best guide books around for families who want to compare the financial aid alternatives."
—*Smart Money*
A one-stop information resource and financial aid adviser featuring in-depth financial aid data and money-saving options at more than 1,500 U.S. four-year colleges and universities. Includes IBM-compatible software for estimating college costs and planning family finances.
ISBN 1-56079-520-4, 720 pp., 81/2 x 11, $26.95 pb, 13th edition

The Ultimate College Survival Guide

Janet Farrar Worthington and Ronald Farrar
Covers everything a college-bound student wants—and needs—to know about college life. It's a "get real" guide to campus life, written in lively, conversational language that hits just the right note with students.
ISBN 1-56079-396-1, 256 pp., 7 x 9, $11.95 pb

USA TODAY Financial Aid for College

Pat Ordovensky
Explains the types of aid available, tells how to qualify for aid, and answers commonly asked questions from *USA TODAY's* annual "Financial Aid and Admissions Hotline."
ISBN 1-56079-568-9, 160 pp., 6 x 9, 8.95 pb, revised edition

Peterson's Professional Degree Programs in the Visual and Performing Arts

Covers more than 800 accredited U.S. institutions, professional music conservatories, and art/design schools that grant undergraduate professional degrees in the areas of studio art, music, theater, and dance.
ISBN 1-56079-281-7, 559 pp., 81/2 x 11, $21.95 pb

**To Order Call:
800-338-3232**

Fax: 609-243-9150

Education for the Earth

". . . a valuable resource." —*Environment Today*
Provides up-to-date, comprehensive profiles of over 200 top college and university environmental studies programs.
ISBN 1-56079-407-0, 327 pp., 7 x 10, $14.95 pb, 2nd edition

**NOW ON THE INTERNET
Peterson's Education Center
http://www.petersons.com**

P Peterson's Princeton, NJ